BRIDGING
COMMUNICATION SKILLS

Sakae Suzuki
Matthew Miller
Patrick McClue

KINSEIDO

Kinseido Publishing Co., Ltd.

3-21 Kanda Jimbo-cho, Chiyoda-ku,
Tokyo 101-0051, Japan

First published 2019 by Kinseido Publishing Co., Ltd.

Design   Nampoosha Co., Ltd.

🎧 音声ファイル無料ダウンロード

http://www.kinsei-do.co.jp/download/4091

**この教科書で 🎧 DL 00 の表示がある箇所の音声は、上記 URL または QR コードにて
無料でダウンロードできます。自習用音声としてご活用ください。**

▶ PC からのダウンロードをお勧めします。スマートフォンなどでダウンロードされる場合は、
ダウンロード前に「解凍アプリ」をインストールしてください。

▶ URL は、**検索ボックスではなくアドレスバー (URL 表示欄)** に入力してください。

▶ お使いのネットワーク環境によっては、ダウンロードできない場合があります。

◎ CD 00   左記の表示がある箇所の音声は、教室用 CD (Class Audio CD) に収録されています。

はしがき

　グローバル化が進む現代では、コミュニケーション能力が必要とされています。特に英語によるコミュニケーション能力は、今後の世界では欠かせないものでしょう。そこでは、英語による簡単な挨拶だけでなく、社会問題や文化的な話題など幅広いトピックについて説明し、意見を述べる英語力が求められます。

　本書は、英語でのディスカッションやプレゼンテーションへと繋がるような基礎的なコミュニケーション力を養う内容で構成されています。

1. 目標
　学生が基本的な英語のコミュニケーション能力を身につけることを目標とし、コミュニケーションに必要な技能が含まれています。最終目標は英語の発信力を身につけることです。

2. 質問とアクティビティ
　4技能に対応した質問とアクティビティが入っています。それぞれ3段階（上級・中級・初級）の内容が含まれています。

3. トピック
　各Unitのトピックについては、日常生活に関する身近な話題から文化的な内容を入れ、それぞれのトピックに関連した言語機能の学習を付けました。

4. Homeworkページ
　各Unitの最後のページに、次のUnitの内容に関するHomeworkをつけました。事前に語彙や表現などを確認してください。

　各Unitには学習目標をつけました。各Unitの活動のねらいは次のとおりです。

Warm-up
　Unitで学習する内容と語彙に関する簡単なアクティビティです。

Reading
　トピックに関連する内容を読み、質問に答えます。次に、AとBに分かれて、それぞれが別の内容について読み、内容を簡単にまとめたり、お互いに質問をしたりして、読んだ内容に関する自分の意見を述べる力をつけます。

Listening
　聴く前に内容に関する質問に答えます。そうすることで聴く内容についての予測ができます。聴きながらメモを取り、テキストにある問題の解答を考えます。

Discussion

読んだり聞いたりした内容について意見交換をし、さらに質問をして回答をまとめます。そうすることで、自分の意見を様々な角度から見直し、最終的な意見へと導きます。

Activity

Unitで得た表現や情報を楽しみながら使う機会を提供します。英語で活動を行うことで実際の言語体験をすることができ、知識を自分のものにすることができるでしょう。

　本書の様々な活動を通して、英語で考え、伝えることへの積極的な姿勢と自信がつき、さらに先へ進むことを願っています。

筆者一同

Foreword

Effective communication skills are required as globalization advances, especially in English. Starting with simple greetings, with this text you will expand your English skills and be able to discuss a wide range of topics such as social problems, cultural topics, and opinions.

This book is composed of contents that cultivate basic communication skills leading to discussions and presentations in English.

1. Goal

The basic goal is for you to acquire English-language skills necessary for communication. Your final goal is to be able to thoroughly convey your thoughts and feelings in English.

2. Questions and Activities

Questions and activities involve practice of all four language skills. This textbook is designed to be adaptable for three levels of classes (advanced, intermediate, and beginner).

3. Topic

Each unit includes cultural content from familiar topics and related language functions.

4. Homework pages

Before each unit is a homework section. Please check the vocabulary and expressions and answer the questions to help you prepare for the topic of the following unit.

The purpose of each unit's activities is as follows.

Warm-up

This is a simple activity introducing the contents and vocabulary.

Reading

You will read text that provides information on the topic and then answer comprehension and expansion questions. Also, you and a partner will read different short texts then briefly summarize what you have learned and express your opinions.

Listening

Before listening, questions are given to allow you to think about the topic beforehand. This will improve your comprehension. Read the comprehension questions and take notes during the listening.

Discussion

Here, you will exchange opinions on the contents, ask further questions, and compile answers. You will review your ideas from various angles and put together your final opinion.

Activity

The activities provide opportunities to use the language and information from the unit in an interesting way. By doing the activity in English, you are gaining real language experience and consolidating your knowledge.

Through the various English activities in this book, we hope that you will become confident in thinking and communicating in English and that you continue to do so even after this course has finished.

The authors

BRIDGING
COMMUNICATION SKILLS

Contents

Introduction I
Getting to know your classmates

☐ Getting to know your classmates
☐ Learning classroom English

Getting to know your classmates

A *Write your answers for questions 1 to 9. Then think of a question for number 10. Get with a partner and ask the 10 questions. Write their answers. Do it again with a new partner.*

		Your answer	Partner 1	Partner 2
1	What's your name?			
2	Where are you from? Where do you live?			
3	What's your major?			
4	Do you have a job? If yes, what do you do?			
5	What do you do in your free time?			
6	What kind of food and drinks do you like?			
7	Can you play a musical instrument or a sport?			
8	What did you do last weekend?			
9	What will you do after this class?			
10				

B *Introduce yourself to a new partner. Tell them about your other partner(s).*

C *Answer these questions. Compare your answers with a partner or group.*

1. Do you have anything in common with your partners?

_____

2. What other questions would you like to ask your partners?

_____

🎧 Listening

A *Listen to two students, Fred and Eri, meeting for the first time. Answer the questions with your partner. Listen again and check your answers.*

🎧 DL 02   💿 CD 02

	Fred	**Eri**
1. Where are they from?		
2. Where do they live?		
3. Who do they live with?		
4. Do they belong to a club?		
5. What do you think they do in their free time?		
6. What do you think they will talk about after class?		

B *The teacher will give you a new partner. Have a conversation similar to Fred and Eri's without using your textbook.*

C *You will hear several short conversations between a student and a teacher. First, cross out the words that are different. Listen again and write the correct words.*

🎧 DL 03   💿 CD 03

Conversation 1

Student: Excuse me, teacher. I have a question.

_____

Teacher: OK. Who's your question?

_____

Student: What is spell your name?

_____

Teacher: It's S-O-L-B-A-N-N. Got it?

Student: I have it. Thank you.

Conversation 2

DL 04   CD 04

Student: I'm sorry for my late.

Teacher: Why you to be late?

Student: I'm missing the bus.

Teacher: OK, don't be careful this time.

Student: I can. Thanks.

Conversation 3

DL 05   CD 05

Student: I'm going to go to the restroom.

Teacher: Where? It is a problem.

Student: Thank you, watch your back.

D *Practice the three conversations with a partner.*

Activity

With a partner, write a conversation using the vocabulary, functions, and information you learned in this unit. Each person should have at least five lines. Practice a few times, then perform in front of the class.

Homework for Unit 2

A *Before the next lesson, you should understand the meanings of these words and phrases. If you are not sure of the meaning, look it up in the dictionary and write its definition.*

Word	Definition	Word	Definition
abroad		frustrated	
to apply		the highlight	
an aquarium		nervous	
comfortable		to organize	
to compare		pressure	
confidence		to remember	
an excursion		to stay late	
fantastic			

B *In the next unit, we will learn about asking and talking about our memories and experiences. Think about your answers to these questions and write down some notes.*

1. Do you have happy memories from high school? What are they?

_____

2. Where did you go for a school trip? How was it?

_____

3. What was studying for the entrance exam like?

_____

C *Exercise on asking and talking about experiences.*

If you are asking about experiences, say …	If you are talking about experiences, say …
What / When / Why / did you …? What about …? How did you feel about / when …?	When I was … I remember that … It was the first time I …

Example

A: What did you do during the long break?

B: I went to Guam. It was the first time I traveled abroad.

Write an example dialogue here

A: _____

B: _____

2 Memories and Experiences

Learning Goal ☐ Asking and talking about experiences

Warm-up

Look at the photo below and answer the following questions with your partner or group.

1. What do you see in the photo? Describe what you see.

   Example *A teacher is speaking and students are looking at the screen.*

2. What was your high school English class like? Describe it.

3. What was the most memorable thing about high school?

4. Did you like your high school?

   Yes, because

   _____.

   No, because

   _____.

Vocabulary

Fill in the blanks with the vocabulary words from the Homework. You may need to change the form of the word to make it fit with the sentence.

1. I feel _____ when I do not know what to do next in class.

2. We are all excited to hear about your _____ in Africa.

3. Although I did not have enough _____, I did my best.

4. I hope that this year is a _____ one for your family.

5. This workshop was _____ by the student committee.

 Reading

Pre-reading: You will read about Hanako's homestay experience in Canada. Talk with your partner or group and imagine what experiences Hanako might have had in Canada. Share with the class.

Read: You have about ten minutes to read and answer the questions below. Then check your answers with your partner or group.

DL 06   CD 06

My experiences in Canada

When I was a first-year high school student, I got a chance to homestay in Canada. I applied for the school program to study English in Vancouver for a month. I had been abroad a few times before then, but it was the first time I stayed in a foreign country for such a long period. I remember that for a couple of days, I was so nervous that I could not speak. After a couple of days though, I began to feel comfortable living with English-speaking people; a host father, a host mother and a host sister. During the day time, I joined some activities organized by a local school. We visited a history museum, Gastown, Vancouver aquarium and the University of British Columbia. When I came home, I talked about what I did with my host family. Gradually, I became used to speaking English. That summer in Canada gave me confidence to use English. It was a fantastic experience for me.

---

1. Where did Hanako do a homestay?

_____

2. How many people were there in Hanako's host family?

_____

3. Name four places Hanako visited.

_____

4. How does Hanako feel about her experiences in Canada?

_____

5. What would you do if an exchange student stayed at your house?

_____

Discussion

Get with a partner and decide who is "A" and who is "B". Student A, go to page 93 and Student B, go to page 94. Read your text and answer the questions. Then explain the most important and interesting points to your partner. After that, have a discussion using the questions below.

1. What made you decide to study at this university/college/junior college?

2. What do you want to study now and why?

3. Some students start their career just after high school. What do you think about that?

4. Do you have a vision for your future job? What is it?

5. What was the most interesting class at high school?

6. Do you think learning English is important? Why or why not?

7. What is your opinion of learning multiple languages?

8. Do you have an experience of speaking English that made you nervous?

9. If you learn multiple languages, what languages would you learn and why?

 # Listening

You will hear Yeona and Kenta talking about their preparation for the entrance exam.

Pre-listening: Before you listen, write how you prepared for the entrance exam when you were a high school student.

DL 09   CD 09

How you prepared for the entrance exam

Listen: Listen and write down what Korean high school students do.

🔴 Korean high school students

Listen again and answer the questions. Check with your partner or group.

1. Did Yeona pass the university entrance exam?

_____

2. How does Yeona feel about being a university student?

_____

3. What is *juku*?

_____

4. What time did Yeona get home when she was a high school student?

_____

5. How do Korean high school students prepare for an entrance exam?

_____

6. What is Jung-Shin good at?

_____

7. What is Yeona good at?

_____

Discussion

Think about your answers to these questions. Then discuss them with your partner or group.

1. What is your opinion about entrance exams?

2. What is your opinion about admission on recommendation?

3. Did you go to *juku*? What was studying at *juku* like?

4. Do you think going to *juku* is necessary to pass entrance exams?

Activity   Asking and talking about experiences

Interview two students in your class about their high school experiences.

Example   What was the highlight of your high school life?

Student A

Student B

In your group of four or five, share the results of the interview.

Highlight of high school life

Homework for Unit 3

Topic	Food and Cooking
Function	Giving instructions / Asking questions

A *Before the next lesson, you should understand the meanings of these words and phrases. If you are not sure of the meaning, look it up in the dictionary and write its definition.*

Word	Definition	Word	Definition
to chop		shredded	
ingredients		a skillet	
organic		to sprinkle	
to preheat		to stir	
produce	food products	a tablespoon	
to season		a teaspoon	
to serve a dish		tender	

B *In the next unit, we will learn about giving cooking instructions. Think about your answers to these questions and write down some notes.*

1. What food do you like?

_____

2. Can you explain how to make tea?

_____

3. What is the name of your favorite restaurant and why do you like it?

_____

4. Imagine you are the owner of a restaurant. Describe your restaurant.

_____

C *Exercise on giving instructions and asking questions.*

If you are giving instructions, say …	If you are asking questions, say …
First …	Could you repeat that, please?
Then …	Did you say …?
After that …	You said, …, right?
Finally …	How do you spell …?

Example

A: First, chop onions and then fry them in a pan.

B: Did you say first chop onions?

Write an example dialogue here

A: _____

B: _____

Food and Cooking

| Learning Goal | ☐ Giving instructions |
| | ☐ Asking questions |

Warm-up

Below is the recipe for a fried egg. Answer the questions below with your partner or group.

A
First, break an egg into a small bowl.

B
After that, pour in the egg.

C
And then, cook the egg until it is white.

D
Finally, season the egg with salt and pepper.

E
Then, put ½ a tablespoon of olive oil in the frying pan.

F
I will show you how to cook a fried egg.

1. What order should the recipe be in? The first step has been done for you.

   (F) ➡ (   ) ➡ (   ) ➡ (   ) ➡ (   ) ➡ (   )

2. What do you usually eat for breakfast?
3. What can you cook?
4. What is your favorite restaurant?
5. Do you think knowing how to cook is important? Why or why not?

Vocabulary

Fill in the blanks with the vocabulary words from the Homework. You may need to change the form of the word to make it fit with the sentence.

1. Flour, sugar … What other _____ do I need to make pancakes?
2. Don't put a cake in a cold oven. First, _____ the oven to 250°.
3. "I prefer _____ produce." "Me too. I don't want chemicals on my food."
4. Add the milk to the eggs and _____ with salt and white pepper.
5. In a large bowl, _____ the milk and sugar until they are blended.

 # Reading

Pre-reading: You will read a recipe to cook a French quiche. Talk with your partner or group and imagine what ingredients you need. Do you think it will be easy or difficult to make a quiche? Share with the class.

Read: You have about ten minutes to read and answer the questions below. Then check your answers with your partner or group.

 Farm Fresh Quiche

This recipe was inspired by talking with farmers in eastern France. It is a wonderful quiche loaded with veggies. Great for vegetarians.

Prep time: 30 minutes
Baking time: 30 minutes

6 servings

Ingredients:

3 tablespoons olive oil, broccoli (cut into florets), onion (chopped), spinach (chopped), 2 garlic cloves, pie sheet, 4 eggs, 1 cup milk, 1 tablespoon dried rosemary, 1 teaspoon salt, 1 teaspoon pepper, 1 cup shredded cheddar cheese or Swiss cheese.

Instructions:

Preheat oven to 350°. In large skillet, heat oil over medium-high heat. Add broccoli and cook until broccoli is tender. Stir in spinach and garlic. Unroll pastry sheet into pie plate. Fill with broccoli mixture.

In bowl, whisk* eggs, milk, rosemary, salt, and pepper. Stir in cheddar cheese. Pour over vegetables. Bake 30 minutes. Let it cool for 15 minutes before cutting.

*whisk: stir quickly

1. What vegetables are in this quiche?

_____

2. How long does it take to make?

_____

3. What is this quiche seasoned with?

_____

4. How many people can eat this dish?

_____

5. How could you change this recipe? What could you add or take out?

_____

6. What other recipes do you know?

_____

Discussion

Get with a partner and decide who is "A" and who is "B". Student A, go to page 95 and read the recipe aloud. Student B takes notes below. Then Student B, go to page 96 and read the recipe aloud. Student A takes notes below. After that, have a discussion using the questions below.

● Recipe notes

Name of the dish	
● Ingredients	
● How to cook (Cooking instructions)	

1. Which recipe (Dum Aloo or Hint of Mint) do you think is the easiest to follow? Why?
2. Which dish would you like to eat? Why?
3. Take turns with your partner explaining the tomato sandwich recipe below.
4. What other recipe can you share with your partner?

# Listening

You will hear a conversation between Samantha Oliver and an interviewer. They are talking about Samantha's career.

▌ *Pre-listening: Before you listen, talk to your partner or group about these questions.*

1. What is your favorite restaurant and why do you like it?

2. What do you know about farmers' markets? Do you have one in your hometown?

▌ *Listen: As you listen, fill in the chart. Then check your answers with your partner or group.*

🎧 DL 13 · ⊙ CD 13

Interview with Samantha Oliver	
1. What is the restaurant's name?	
2. Where is the restaurant?	
3. Where did she fall in love with cooking?	
4. Why is there no menu at her restaurant?	
5. How did she learn to cook?	
6. Why do you think she buys her ingredients at a farmers' market?	
7. Why does she have only one restaurant?	

Listen again and answer the questions. Check with your partner or group.

1. When did she go to France as a student?

———————————————————————————————

2. What does she believe about organic produce?

———————————————————————————————

3. Why do you think it is difficult to reserve a table at her restaurant?

———————————————————————————————

4. What does Samantha mean when she says, "food creates family"?

———————————————————————————————

Discussion

Think about your answers to these questions. Then discuss them with your partner or group.

1. What is organic food? What is your opinion about it?

2. What is good about going to a farmers' market? How are farmers' markets different from supermarkets?

3. Samantha said, "We are what we eat". Discuss what she means and express your opinion.

4. What do you think about Samantha's philosophy about food?

Activity   Giving instructions and Asking questions

Design your own restaurant using the chart below.

Restaurant's name:
_____

Location:
_____

Special dishes on the menu:
_____

What makes your restaurant unique?
_____

Ask your partner questions below.

1. What is the name of your restaurant?
2. What made you choose the name of the restaurant?
3. Where is the restaurant located? How can you go there?
4. What are special dishes of your restaurant?
5. How is the restaurant unique?
6. How do you cook the special dishes?

Homework for Unit 4

Topic	Health
Function	Asking for and giving advice

A *Before the next lesson, you should understand the meanings of these words and phrases. If you are not sure of the meaning, look it up in the dictionary and write its definition.*

Word	Definition	Word	Definition
allergic		the immune system	
a fad diet		a lifestyle change	
fatigue		nutritious	
fitness		to prevent	
the flu		a symptom	
a habit		a treatment	

B *In the next unit, we will learn about being healthy. Think about your answers to these questions and write down some notes.*

1. Are you or someone you know allergic to anything?

_____

2. When you have a cold, what symptoms do you usually have?

_____

3. When you have a cold, what treatments do you take?

_____

4. What do you do to prevent illnesses?

_____

5. What are your fitness and eating habits?

_____

C *Exercise on asking for and giving advice.*

If you are asking for advice, say …	If you are giving advice, say …
What should I do?	You should …
What do you suggest?	I suggest …
What would you do?	If I were you, I'd …
What do you advise?	You'd better …

Example

A: I can't wake up on time in the morning, so I'll set three alarms. What would you do?

B: If I were you, I'd go to bed earlier.

Write an example dialogue here

A: _____

B: _____

Health

Warm-up

Look at the photos below and answer the following questions with your partner or group. Try to use the phrases from **C** *of the Homework.*

1. What are the images in the photos?
2. Which ones are healthy? Which ones are not healthy?
3. What advice would you give someone doing the unhealthy ones?
4. What do you do that is healthy?

Vocabulary

Fill in the blanks with the vocabulary words from the Homework. You may need to change the form of the word to make it fit with the sentence.

1. I am _____ to cats. I sneeze and get a runny nose when I am near them.

2. Drinking tea with honey is a good _____ for a sore throat.

3. Before running, I do stretches to _____ muscle aches.

4. I am so busy, so I have a bad _____ of eating food from the convenience store. It is cheap, but not very _____.

5. _____ that includes more sleep will improve your _____.

 Reading

Pre-reading: You will read about a common health problem. Talk with your partner or group and imagine some common illnesses. Share with the class.

Read: You have about ten minutes to read and answer the questions below. Then check your answers with your partner or group.

 DL 14   CD 14

Visiting a Doctor

Ken woke up in the morning feeling awful again. His throat was sore. He had a headache, a fever, and a bad cough. Although he slept for a long time, he still felt fatigued. He decided to go to the hospital and visit his doctor.

The doctor asked Ken what his symptoms were and how long he had them. Ken told the doctor that he first started feeling ill a week ago. The doctor took Ken's temperature, listened to his breathing, and examined his throat. The doctor asked Ken if he was allergic to anything, and Ken said that he wasn't.

The doctor told Ken that he had the flu. The treatment the doctor suggested was for Ken to take some medicine, get plenty of rest, and drink lots of water. He also advised to come back to the clinic if the symptoms did not get better after a few days.

Ken asked the doctor if he could give him advice about how to prevent getting sick in the future. The doctor said that Ken should eat healthy meals, sleep well, wash his hands more often, and avoid stress. Doing these things may not stop Ken from getting sick but having a healthy body at the start will help fight the flu, and the symptoms may not be as bad or last as long.

Ken thanked the doctor, got his medicine, and went back home to bed.

1. What are Ken's symptoms?

_____

2. How many days has Ken been ill?

_____

3. What medical tests did the doctor give him?

_____

4. What is the doctor's treatment for the flu?

_____

5. When and why should Ken go back to see the doctor?

_____

6. What advice did the doctor give Ken about staying healthy?

_____

7. Tell your partner about the last time you went to the doctor or dentist.

_____

Discussion

Get with a partner and decide who is "A" and who is "B". Student A, go to page 97 and Student B, go to page 98. Read and answer your questions. Then explain the most important and interesting points to your partner. After that, have a discussion using the questions below.

1. Do you or anyone you know suffer from any of these allergies?

2. What treatment is there for people who suffer from allergies?

3. What in your life is stressful?

4. What do you do to release stress?

5. How much sleep do you usually get a night? Is it enough? How much sleep do you think you need?

 Listening

You will hear about some lifestyle changes that can lead to better health.

| Pre-listening: Before you listen, talk to your partner or group about these questions.

1. What are some good health habits you have?
2. What are some bad health habits you have?
3. Have you ever tried a fad diet? If so, which one?

| Listen: As you listen, fill in the gaps with the missing phrases.

DL 17   CD 17

1	Instead, making _____ in the way you live will create good habits that will stay with you for the _____ your life.
2	Try using the stairs instead of the elevator to walk as much as you can _____.
3	However, it's also high in calories without having much _____.
4	Getting a _____ makes you ready to have a productive day.
5	You won't _____ overnight, but these changes will benefit your health _____.

Listen again and answer the questions. Check with your partner or group.

1. Is going to the gym necessary to keep active?

_____

2. How much activity does a person need to improve fitness?

_____

3. Besides fresh fruit and vegetables, what are other examples of nutritious food?

_____

4. What are the benefits of getting good sleep?

_____

Discussion

Think about your answers to these questions. Then discuss them with a new partner or group.

1. What are some good health habits you have?
2. Have you ever tried a fad diet? If so, which one?
3. What do you want to change about your health?

Activity | Asking for and giving advice

Think about some lifestyle changes you would like to make to improve your health and fitness. Write the three changes you would like to make below. Then ask your classmates to give you advice on how you can make the changes. Look at the expressions in C *of the Homework.*

Change 1	
Student 1	
Student 2	
Student 3	
Student 4	
Student 5	

Change 2	
Student 1	
Student 2	
Student 3	
Student 4	
Student 5	

Change 3	
Student 1	
Student 2	
Student 3	
Student 4	
Student 5	

Topic ● **Humans and Animals**

Function ● **Expressing opinions / Agreeing and disagreeing**

A *Before the next lesson, you should understand the meanings of these words and phrases. If you are not sure of the meaning, look it up in the dictionary and write its definition.*

Word	Definition	Word	Definition
a cage		to raise (an animal)	
cruel / cruelty		texture	
to have empathy		unique	
hypocritical		a vegetarian	
an investigator	a detective	vegetarianism	
nutrition		a vet	
to prefer		a zoologist	

B *In the next unit, we will learn about humans and animals. Think about your answers to these questions and write down some notes.*

1. Do you have a pet? If no, would you like to have one? Why or why not?

_____

2. What is your favorite book or movie that has an animal in it?

_____

3. Do you eat meat? If yes, what kinds of meat? If no, why not?

_____

4. Do you like going to zoos or aquariums? Why or why not?

_____

5. What is your opinion about how humans use animals (for food, protection, entertainment, sport, transportation, etc.)?

_____

_____

C *Exercise on expressing opinions, agreeing, and disagreeing.*

Express opinions	Agree	Disagree
I think …	I agree.	I disagree.
I believe …	I think so, too.	No, I don't think so.
I suppose …	You're right.	No way.
In my opinion …	Yes, exactly.	I see what you mean, but …

Example

A: Do you agree that humans should be vegetarians?

B: It's better for the environment so I sort of agree, but I don't think it's realistic.

Write an example dialogue here

A: _____

B: _____

Humans and Animals

Warm-up

Look at the photos below and answer the following questions with your partner or group.

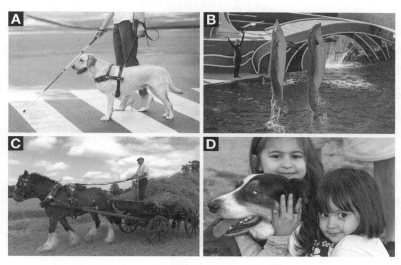

1. What are the animals doing in each photo?
2. How do humans use the animals in each photo?
3. Do you have a pet or work with animals? If no, would you like to?
4. What ways do humans use animals? Make a list.

    Examples   *food, protection, sport, transportation, etc.*

Vocabulary

Fill in the blanks with the vocabulary words from the Homework. You may need to change the form of the word to make it fit with the sentence.

1. I think it is _____ to put animals in cages because they are not happy.
2. She became a vet because she _____ for animals and wanted to help them.
3. Sheila's family _____ sheep on their farm. They use the sheep's wool for sweaters.
4. The senbei was old so its _____ was soft, not crispy.
5. The _____ studied the crime and found the thief.

 # Reading

Pre-reading: *You will read about the different reasons some people are vegetarians. Talk with your partner or group and imagine at least two reasons people might not eat meat. Share with the class.*

Read: *You have about ten minutes to read and answer the questions below. Then check your answers with your partner or group.*

🎧 DL 18   💿 CD 18

Vegetarianism

It is a fact that many humans eat animals. Some people eat them for nutrition and others eat them because, in their opinion, animal meat tastes good. However, vegetarians do not eat animals at all. Surprisingly, there are many reasons. Religion, environment, health, and taste are just four of these reasons.

Some people do not eat meat because of their religion. Some religions, like Jainism, believe that all animals have a soul. They believe we should not kill or harm any living creature.

We know that raising animals for food damages the environment. Animal farms can cause a lot of air and water pollution. Thus, some people choose to become vegetarians to help protect the environment.

Other vegetarians choose not to eat meat for their health. They suppose that by eating less fat, they will be healthier. It is true that vegetarians have less risk of heart disease, but they must be careful to get enough vitamins like B12.

Finally, some people are vegetarians simply because they do not like the taste, smell, or texture of meat. These people prefer eating vegetables and fruit because, in their opinion, they taste better.

1. Why do some people eat meat?

_____

2. What do some religions believe about eating meat?

_____

3. Why do some people think that vegetarianism is good for the environment?

_____

4. Do you think being a vegetarian is healthier? Why or why not?

_____

5. Do you eat meat? If no, why not? If yes, what kinds of meat do you like and dislike?

_____

6. Do you believe that there are some kinds of animals humans should not eat? Look at the photos below and draw a line between what you think are pets and food.

_____

pets ▶ ▶ ▶ ▶ ▶ ▶ ▶ ▶ ▶ ▶ ▶ ▶ ▶ ▶ ▶ ▶ ▶ ▶ food

Discussion

Get with a partner and decide who is "A" and who is "B". Student A, go to page 99 and Student B, go to page 100. Read your text and answer the questions. Then explain the most important and interesting points to your partner. After that, have a discussion using the questions below.

1. For you, what was the most interesting thing about the Humans and Animals reading?
2. What is your favorite kind of animal? Why do you like them?
3. What animals do you not like? Why do you not like them?
4. Would you like to work with animals? If yes, what kind of job? If no, why not?
5. Do you have a pet? If no, would you like a pet?
6. What are the good and bad things about having a pet?
7. What is your opinion about testing drugs on animals?
8. What is your opinion about using animals to make leather bags and fur coats?
9. Do you prefer cats, dogs, birds, or fish? Why?
10. What can children learn by having a pet?
11. What are some unusual or unique pets?

Listening

You will hear Susan invite Toshi to the zoo and to a vegetarian restaurant. However, Toshi does not want to go ...

Pre-listening: Before you listen, talk to your partner about this question: Why do you think Toshi does not want to go to the zoo?

Listen: As you listen, decide whether Susan and Toshi agree or disagree with the following opinions. Mark ○ if they agree or ✕ if they disagree. Check with your partner or group. Then fill in the chart for your opinion.

DL 21   CD 21

Opinions	Susan	Toshi	You
1. Animals should not be in cages.			
2. The animals in a zoo are free.			
3. Animals have better lives in a zoo.			
4. Zoos can be educational.			
5. Zoos smell horrible.			

Post-listening: Now ask your partner for their opinions. For example, "Animals should not be in cages. Do you agree or disagree?"

Listen again and answer the questions. Check with your partner or group.

1. What does Toshi think about zoos?

_____

2. What is Susan's opinion about zoos?

_____

3. Why did Susan's sister want to become a vet?

_____

4. What are two things that Susan and Toshi agree about?

_____

5. What does Susan mean when she says the zoo animals are "free from hunters and sickness"?

_____

6. Why does Susan think Toshi is being hypocritical?

_____

7. Would you go to the zoo with Susan? Why or why not?

_____

8. Would you go to the vegetarian restaurant? Why or why not?

_____

Discussion

Think about your answers to these questions. Then discuss them with your partner or group.

1. What is your opinion about zoos?
2. What do you think about vegetarianism?
3. Humans use animals for food, clothing, entertainment, transportation, sport, protection, drug testing, and as pets. What is your opinion about how we use animals in each of these ways?

Activity Agreeing and disagreeing

Walk around the room and ask each survey question to ten of your classmates. Mark how many agree and disagree. Add your own question for number 6.

Example

A: Do you agree that humans should be vegetarians?

B: It's better for the environment, so I sort of agree, but I don't think it's realistic.

And then, report your research to your group.

Example

A: 40% of our class agrees that humans should be vegetarians.

Opinions	Disagree completely	Agree a little	Agree completely
1. Humans should be vegetarians.			
2. It is a valuable experience to have a pet.			
3. Putting animals in zoos is cruel.			
4. Killing animals to make fur coats is ok.			
5. It would be fun to work with animals.			
6.			

Now, use the following questions for discussion.

1. What was the most interesting or surprising thing you found from the survey?
2. How do you think the survey results would change if you asked older people?
3. How do you think the survey results would change if you asked foreigners?

☑ **Agree**
☐ **Disagree**

Homework for Unit 6

Topic	Telling Stories
Function	Storytelling and reacting

A *Before the next lesson, you should understand the meanings of these words and phrases. If you are not sure of the meaning, look it up in the dictionary and write its definition.*

Word	Definition	Word	Definition
ashamed		huge	
a character	a person in a story	in the middle of nowhere	far away from other places
conceited		Krakow, Poland	
exhausted		the setting	place and time of the story
a fable		tons of	
to grab		upset	unhappy, worried

B *In the next unit, we will learn about telling stories. Think about your answers to these questions and write down some notes.*

1. What kind of stories do you prefer (funny, romantic, scary, science fiction, fantasy, non-fiction, historical, etc.)?

_____

2. What is one of your favorite stories?

_____

3. What traditional Japanese stories, fables, or ghost stories do you know?

_____

4. What is something interesting, embarrassing, or frightening that has happened to you or someone you know?

_____

C *Exercise on storytelling and reacting.*

If you are telling a story, say ...	If you are reacting, say ...
You'll never believe what happened ... Guess what. One time ... When I was ... First ... Then ... After that ... Finally ...	Tell me what happened. Oh, really? What happened after that? I bet.* I can imagine.*

*These phrases show that you understand the speaker's feeling.

Example

You'll never believe what happened on the train last night.

Write two examples here

1. _____

2. _____

6 Telling Stories

☐ Storytelling and reacting

Warm-up

Look at the picture below and, using your imagination, do 1-4 with your partner or group. When you tell the story, try to use the phrases from **C** *of the Homework.*

1. Who are the characters?
2. Where are they?
3. What happened first? Then what happened? What finally happened?
4. You and your partner tell your story to another pair or group.

Vocabulary

Fill in the blanks with the vocabulary words from the Homework. You may need to change the form of the word to make it fit with the sentence.

1. The main _____ in Peter Rabbit is a young boy rabbit.

2. He is very proud of himself, but he should not be so _____ because he is not better than everyone else.

3. When the boy was caught stealing candy, he felt guilty and was very

    _____.

4. There were _____ people on the train in the morning so it was difficult to get on.

5. My grandparents' house is _____. There are no stores or houses nearby and it is difficult to travel to without a car.

 **Reading**

Pre-reading: You will read a fable from the country of Madagascar. It is a story about a proud boar and a smart chameleon. Talk with your partner or group and imagine what might happen in the story. Share with the class.

Read: You have about ten minutes to read and answer the questions below. Then check your answers with your partner or group.

🎧 DL 22   💿 CD 22

The Boar and the Chameleon

A big brown boar, running through the forest, saw a long green chameleon moving slowly across a tree branch. The boar laughed at him and said, "You're weak and slow! Look at me! I'm strong and fast!"

The chameleon smiled and replied, "Don't be so conceited. I'm strong and fast too, but in a different way."

The boar loudly laughed. "If you're so strong and fast, then let's race to the top of this hill."

"Alright, let's race. Ready? Set. Go!" yelled the chameleon. Just as the boar started running, the smart little chameleon grabbed the tail of the boar.

When the boar got to the top of the small hill, he turned around and said, "Where are you chameleon? You're so far behind I can't even see you."

The chameleon let go of the boar's tail, fell to the ground, and said, "I'm right behind you. I've been waiting here a long time."

The boar was so surprised, then felt ashamed. "I'm sorry that I didn't believe you, my little friend. I don't know how you won the race, but now I know you are stronger and faster than I am. I was a fool not to believe you."

1. Who are the two characters in this story? What do they look like? How do they act?

---

2. What is the setting of this story?

---

3. Why did the characters have a race? Who won the race? How did they win?

40

4. How did the boar feel at the end of the story?

_____

5. What lessons do we learn from this fable?

_____

6. Imagine the chameleon apologizes to the boar for lying and tricking him. What do you think the boar says?

_____

7. What are some fables that you know?

_____

Discussion

Get with a partner and decide who is "A" and who is "B". Student A, go to page 101 and Student B, go to page 102. Read your text and answer the questions. Then tell the story to your partner. After that, have a group discussion using the questions below.

1. Which story did you like the best, *An Embarrassing Mistake* or *A Frightening Bus Ride*? Why?

2. What kind of stories do you prefer (funny, romantic, scary, science fiction, fantasy, non-fiction, historical, etc.)?

3. What is one of your favorite stories?

4. Do you know of any traditional Japanese stories or fables? Tell it in English to your group.

5. Why do you think people enjoy telling and listening to stories?

6. Tell a funny, interesting, or surprising story about yourself or someone you know.

# Listening

You will hear Mana talking to JP, her friend from work. JP took a trip to Poland during the summer and something surprising happened on his trip.

Pre-listening: Before you listen, talk to your partner or group about these questions.

1. What do you think JP did in Poland?
2. What surprising thing do you think happened to JP?

Listen: As you listen, put the following phrases in order.   DL 25   CD 25

	He ran to catch the last bus back to the city.
	JP knew he was on the wrong bus.
1	He took a bus from Krakow into the countryside to visit a huge church.
	He fell asleep on the bus.
	The bus driver woke him up.
	He followed the river back to Krakow.

Listen again and answer the questions. Check with your partner or group.

1. How was JP's trip? _____
2. Did he go to Warsaw and Krakow? _____
3. What is special about the center of Krakow? _____
4. Why did JP take a bus to the countryside? _____
5. What problem did he have? _____
6. How do you think JP felt? _____
7. How did JP solve the problem? _____
8. What happened in the end? _____
9. What do you think JP did after he returned to his hotel?

   _____

10. JP said the center of Krakow is "quite touristy". Does he mean it in a positive or negative way? What do you think he means?

    _____

Discussion

Think about your answers to these questions. Then discuss them with your partner or group.

1. When you travel, do you prefer to go somewhere touristy or to a place that is in the middle of nowhere? Why?

2. When you travel, do you prefer to go to markets, historical buildings, shops, cafes, or other places?

3. Are you interested in visiting World Heritage Sites? Why or why not?

4. Have you ever been lost? What happened?

Activity   Storytelling

With a partner, write a story using the vocabulary, functions, and information you learned in this unit. Think about the characters—what they look like and how they feel. Think about the setting, the action, and the ending. Tell your story to the class.

_____

_____

_____

_____

_____

_____

_____

_____

_____

_____

_____

_____

_____

Topic ● **Emotions**
Function ● **Describing feelings and emotions**

A *Before the next lesson, you should understand the meanings of these words and phrases. If you are not sure of the meaning, look it up in the dictionary and write its definition.*

Word	Definition	Word	Definition
to annoy		frustration	
a charity		irrational	
confusion		irritation	
depression		pet peeve	
disgust		phobia	
to exaggerate		relief	

B *In the next unit, we will learn about describing feelings and emotions. Think about your answers to these questions and write down some notes.*

1. What makes you happy? What makes you sad?

2. Do you usually show your emotions, or do you keep them hidden?

3. Do you have a phobia? If so, what is it?

4. What is your pet peeve?

C *Exercise on describing feelings and emotions.*

If you are asking about someone's feelings, say ...	If you are explaining your feelings, say ...
How are you feeling? What's the matter? How do you feel about ...?	I feel ... I'm ...

If someone has a positive feeling	If someone has a negative feeling
I'm glad to hear that.	I'm sorry to hear that.

Example

A: What's the matter?

B: I feel worried because I lost my favorite ring.

A: I'm sorry to hear that.

Write an example dialogue here

A: _____

B: _____

A: _____

Learning Goal ☐ Describing feelings and emotions

Warm-up

With a partner, brainstorm a list of emotions. What emotions are being shown in the photos below?

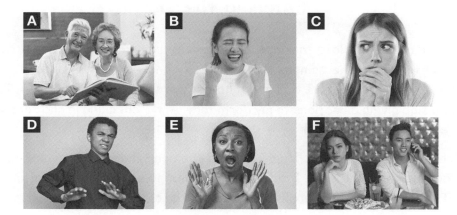

1. Which are positive emotions?
2. Which are negative emotions?
3. Do you always show your emotions?
4. How do you know what someone feels when they do not say anything? Give examples.
5. Why do humans have negative emotions like fear and anger?

Vocabulary

Fill in the blanks with the vocabulary words from the Homework. You may need to change the form of the word to make it fit with the sentence.

1. This train station is very _____. I always get lost because there are so many lines and exits.
2. What a _____! I thought I lost my ring, but it was in my bag.
3. The movie was about endangered animals. It was really _____.
4. I have a _____ of insects. I cannot even look at a photo of a bug.
5. People making loud chewing sounds when they eat is my biggest _____.

 Reading

Pre-reading: You will read a diary entry about Sara's first day in the dormitory. Do you live in a dorm? How was your first day there? If you do not live in a dorm, how would you feel about living in one? Discuss with your partner or group.

Read: You have about ten minutes to read and answer the questions below. Then check your answers with your partner or group.

 DL 26   CD 26

Entering the Dorm

I arrived on campus late this morning. There were many first-year students arriving today, so the campus was very busy and confusing. I didn't know where anything was, and I was about to get worried about what to do. Then I saw a sign giving directions to my dormitory. After checking in and receiving my keys, I went to my room.

My room was on the third floor. I opened the door and was surprised to see the boxes that I had sent. I didn't expect them to be in my room waiting for me. That was a relief. It would have been hard to bring the boxes up myself since there was no elevator.

When I closed the door, I saw my roommate sitting on one of the beds. She had a friendly smile and I felt comfortable with her right away. Her name is Sachie and I was surprised to learn that not only is she from Tokyo, but her family lives about 30 minutes away by train! She said she wanted to have a full university life and didn't want to commute to school. Trains are so crowded in the morning, so I could understand that.

I'm from another part of the country. Although I've just arrived, I already miss my family. I envy Sachie that she can see her family anytime she likes. Sachie said she can introduce fun places in the city to me. I look forward to getting to know Sachie better.

---

1. How did Sara feel when she arrived on campus?

_____

2. Why was she glad that the boxes were in her room?

_____

3. How did Sara feel about Sachie when she first met her?

_____

4. What surprised her about Sachie?

_____

5. How does Sara feel about her family?

_____

6. Why does Sara envy Sachie?

_____

7. How do you think the roommates will feel about each other later in the semester?

_____

8. Which do you think is better, living in a dormitory or living with family?

_____

Discussion

Get with a partner and decide who is "A" and who is "B". Student A, go to page 103 and Student B, go to page 104. Read your text and answer the questions. Then explain the most important and interesting points to your partner. After that, have a discussion using the questions below.

1. What words in your language make you annoyed when you hear them?

2. What are your pet peeves?

3. Do you or anyone you know have a phobia?

4. How can you overcome the fear of speaking in front of a large group of people?

Listening

You will hear about how countries measure their people's happiness. This is called World Happiness Index.

▌ *Pre-listening: Before you listen, talk to your partner about these questions.*

1. Are you a happy person?

2. Do you think some countries are happier than others?

3. Do you think happiness can be measured?

▌ *Listen: As you listen, fill in the gaps with the missing phrases.*

DL 29   CD 29

1	However, another way of looking at success is by measuring _____ about their countries.
2	In 1972, the 4th King of Bhutan said, "_____ is more important than Gross National Product."
3	In 2011, the UN asked countries to measure the happiness of its people based on (1) _____, (3) how much support they get _____, (5) _____ businesses and government.
4	People around the world were given a survey and asked to _____ on a scale of 0 (worst) to 10 (best).
5	Since the first report in 2012, Denmark, Finland, Iceland and Norway have been at the _____.

Listen again and answer the questions. Check with your partner or group.

1. What are the other three types of questions people were asked on the survey?

(2) _____

(4) _____

(6) _____

2. How often is the World Happiness Index published?

_____

3. Why do you think the top countries scored high on the happiness index?

_____

Discussion

Think about your answers to these questions. Then discuss them with your partner or group.

1. Are you a happy person?
2. Do you think happiness can be measured?
3. Look at the six types of survey questions. Which ones are the most important for your happiness? Why?

Activity   Describing feelings and emotions

With your partner, choose an emotion and make three questions you can ask to measure that emotion. For example, you can make questions about excitement or fear. Write your three questions below. Ask your classmates to answer on a scale of 0 (worst) to 10 (best) and explain why. Use the expressions in C of the Homework to respond to your classmate's reason.

Question 1	
Student 1	
Student 2	
Student 3	
Student 4	
Student 5	

Question 2	
Student 1	
Student 2	
Student 3	
Student 4	
Student 5	

Question 3	
Student 1	
Student 2	
Student 3	
Student 4	
Student 5	

8

Introduction II
Talking about summer break

| Learning Goal | ☐ Talking about summer break |
| | ☐ Review of speaking and listening skills |

Talking about summer break

A *Write your answers to the following questions in English. Think of one more question. Then ask a partner the questions.*

		Your answer	Partner 1	Partner 2
1	What's your name?			
2	How was your summer break?			
3	Did you travel anywhere during the summer?			
4	Did you work during the summer?			
5	Did you meet any old friends or make any new ones?			
6	What did you enjoy eating and drinking during the summer?			
7	Did you use English at all during the break?			
8	Did you see any movies or read any books?			
9	Did you go to the mountains or the beach?			
10	Are you happy to be back at school?			
11				

B *Introduce yourself to a new partner. Tell them about your other partner(s).*

Answer these questions. Compare your answers with a partner or group.

1. Do you have anything in common with your partners?

_____

2. What other questions would you like to ask your partners?

_____

🎧 Listening

A Listen to two students, Fred and Eri, talking about their summer break. Answer the questions with your partner. Listen again and check your answers.

🎧 DL 30   💿 CD 30

	Fred	Eri
1. How was their summer break?		
2. Where did they go?		
3. Who did they travel with?		
4. What did they do on their trips?		
5. Did they work during the summer?		
6. Are they happy to be back at school?		

B The teacher will give you a new partner. Have a conversation similar to Fred and Eri's without using your textbook.

C You will hear several short conversations about summer break. First, cross out the words that are different. Listen again and write the correct words.

🎧 DL 31   💿 CD 31

Conversation 1

Student:	Hey, Sullivan. How do your summer?
	_____
Teacher:	Great, thanks. How about you?
	_____
Student:	It was terrible.
	_____
Teacher:	What do you mean?
	_____
Student:	I was part-time job, but I went on the beach a couple times.
	_____

Conversation 2

🎧 DL 32   💿 CD 32

Student 1:   What did you do in summer vacation?

_____

Student 2:   I go to an English school the Philippines.

_____

Student 1:   No say! That was awesome.

_____

Student 2:   Yeah, it was a precious treasure. Did you get up to anything?

_____

Student 1:   I go driving school. I finally got driver's license!

_____

Conversation 3

🎧 DL 33   💿 CD 33

Student: Long time no see! Did you good in summer?

_____

Teacher: It was ok. I just went Sendai see parents.

_____

Student: That shaved ice. Is your hometown in Miyagi?

_____

Teacher: No, my hometown is Saga, but my family moved the cheer.

_____

D *Practice the three conversations with a partner.*

Activity

With a partner, write a conversation between two students talking about their summer breaks. Use the vocabulary, functions, and information you learned in this unit. Each person should have at least seven lines. Practice a few times, then perform in front of the class.

_____

_____

_____

_____

_____

_____

_____

Homework for Unit 9

Topic ● **Intelligence**

Function ● **Asking for information / Clarifying**

A *Before the next lesson, you should understand the meanings of these words and phrases. If you are not sure of the meaning, look it up in the dictionary and write its definition.*

Word	Definition	Word	Definition
to assess		an intuition	
a dialogue		I.Q.	
to explore		logical	
to identify		multiple	
independent		a psychologist	
to insist		to reason	
interpersonal		a will	desire or wish
intrapersonal			

B *In the next unit, we will learn about intelligence. Think about your answers to these questions and write down some notes.*

1. Are you good at playing the piano or playing tennis?

_____

2. Who is your role model and why?

_____

3. What is your image of being intelligent?

_____

4. What is your opinion about testing intelligence?

_____

C *Exercise on asking for information and clarifying.*

If you are asking for information, say ...	If you are clarifying, say ...
What did you say?	So, your idea is ...
What do you mean by ...?	So, you think ...
I'm not following you. Could you repeat that, please?	What I mean is ...
	What I wanted to say was ...
What's ... about?	You mean ...?

Examples

What do you mean by multiple intelligences?
What I wanted to say was (that) I trusted him.

Write two examples here

1. _____

2. _____

9 Intelligence

Learning Goal

☐ Asking for information
☐ Clarifying

Warm-up

Each type describes one kind of intelligence. Choose the type which describes you.

Type A
- I enjoy math and using numbers.
- I keep a 'things to do' list.
- I enjoy solving logic problems.

Type B
- I can sense the moods and feelings of others.
- I work best when interacting with people.
- I prefer group activities rather than ones I do alone.

Type C
- I enjoy doing jigsaw, maze and/or other visual puzzles.
- I read charts and maps easily.
- I have a good sense of direction.

Type D
- I know myself well.
- I am not easily influenced by other people.
- I have a good understanding of my feelings and how I will react to situations.

Type E
- I often play music in my mind.
- My mood changes when I listen to music.
- It is easy for me to follow the beat of music.
- I can remember pieces of music easily.

Type F
- I can recognize many animals and plants.
- I am sensitive to the environment and nature. I am aware of weather changes.

Type G
- I like working with my hands.
- I prefer to be physically involved rather than sitting.

1. Which type do you belong to and why do you think so?
2. Which type belongs to musical intelligence?
3. What does each type describe? Think about names for each type.
4. Ask four students which type they belong to and why they think so.

Vocabulary

Fill in the blanks with the vocabulary words from the Homework. You may need to change the form of the word to make it fit with the sentence.

1. _____ study people's behaviors and emotions.
2. Scientists have _____ causes of the earthquake.
3. He had an _____ that there was something wrong.
4. Hanako has a strong _____ to finish this job.
5. After graduating university, she became _____ of her parents.

 Reading

Pre-reading: You will read on multiple intelligences. According to Howard Gardner, an American psychologist, there are the seven intelligences. Talk with your partner or group and imagine what the seven intelligences are. Share with the class.

Read: You have about ten minutes to read and answer the questions below. Then check your answers with your partner or group.

DL 34 CD 34

What is intelligence?

The definition of intelligence has been tested by standardized I.Q. or aptitude tests which are based on skills such as verbal fluency, wide vocabulary and so on. Those tests assess people's abilities by the same categories: that is one interpretation of intelligence.

Howard Gardner, a psychologist at Harvard university, however, identified seven intelligences. He insisted that people have different abilities to solve a problem or create a product that is valued in a society. Gardner was sure that there are more intelligences than those assessed by I.Q. tests and typically valued in school.

People with visual-spatial intelligence have a strong sense of space as do architects and sailors. They are good at reading texts with graphs, charts and pictures.

People with bodily intelligence have a keen sense of body awareness as do dancers and surgeons. They like movement, making things and are good at communication through body language.

People with musical intelligence are sensitive to sounds and environments. They can learn with tools such as musical instruments, music, and multimedia.

People with interpersonal intelligence understand and interact with others. They have many friends. They like group activities and dialogues.

People with intrapersonal intelligence understand their own interests and goals. They tend to shy away from others and be independent. They have intuition, a strong will, confidence and opinions.

People with logical-mathematical intelligence like reasoning and calculating. They are good at exploring patterns and relationships and like to experiment.

People with naturalistic intelligence are sensitive to the environment and nature. They like walking in the woods and planting flowers.

1. How is intelligence sometimes tested?

_____

2. Who is Howard Gardner?

_____

3. What are people with bodily intelligence good at?

_____

4. Why do you think people with interpersonal intelligence have many friends?

_____

5. What kind of person might make a good zoologist? Why?

_____

Discussion

Get with a partner and decide who is "A" and who is "B". Student A, go to page 105 and Student B, go to page 106. Read your text and answer the questions. Then explain the most important and interesting points to your partner. After that, have a group discussion using the questions below.

1. Do you believe that blood type explains what people are? Why or why not?
2. When and how did you find your blood type?
3. Do you know anyone who matches blood type A? Why do you think so?
4. Do you know anyone who matches blood type O? Why do you think so?
5. Do you know anyone who matches blood type B? Why do you think so?
6. Do you know anyone who matches blood type AB? Why do you think so?
7. How do colors affect your daily life?
8. Why do you think fire engines are red in Japan?
9. Why do you think traffic lights have three colors?
10. How do colors of products affect customers? Examples?

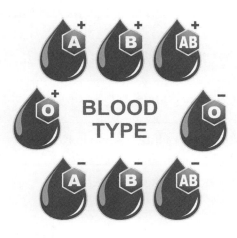

Listening

You will hear a conversation between Sachiko and James. They are talking about a part-time job.

▌ *Pre-listening: Before you listen, talk to your partner about these questions.*

1. What kind of part-time job have you experienced?
2. What do you think is the best way to communicate with children?

▌ *Listen: As you listen, fill in the chart.*　　🎧 DL 37　💿 CD 37

What does Howard Gardner say?

Where does James work?

Who are James' students?

What is James' intelligence type?

What is Sachiko's intelligence type?

Listen again and answer the questions. Check with your partner or group.

1. About how long have James and Sachiko not seen each other?

_____

2. What class did they take together?

_____

3. How does James' school divide its students into groups?

_____

4. What type of intelligence is Keiko?

_____

5. How does Keiko teach English?

_____

Discussion

Think about your answers to these questions. Then discuss them with your partner or group.

1. What do you think about the theory of multiple intelligences?
2. Are there more intelligences we should add to Gardner's multiple intelligences?
3. What intelligence do the following people have and why?

a. Shohei Ohtani		**e.** Vincent Van Gogh
b. Bill Gates		**f.** Walt Disney
c. Haruki Murakami		**g.** Taylor Swift
d. Sota Fujii		**h.** Marie Kondo

Activity | Asking for information

Walk around the room and ask eight of your classmates one of the survey questions below to find out their personality. Write their names in the appropriate blanks. Try to find at least one person for each personality type.

Example

A: When you travel, do you usually have an exact plan?

B: Yes, I do.

A: You are organized.

Personality Survey

Questions	Answers/Personalities
1. When you travel, do you usually have an exact plan?	**Yes:** organized **No:** adventurous
2. In the future, do you want to work for a large company or start your own business?	**Large company:** a team-player **Own business:** self-reliant
3. Do you prefer hanging out with old friends or meeting new people?	**Old friends:** faithful **New people:** sociable
4. Would you prefer to have a roommate or to live alone?	**Roommate:** friendly **Live alone:** independent

Personality	Name	Personality	Name
Organized		Faithful	
Adventurous		Sociable	
A team-player		Friendly	
Self-reliant		Independent	

Homework for Unit 10

Topic ● **Superstitions**
Function ● **Expressing beliefs and abstract ideas**

A *Before the next lesson, you should understand the meanings of these words and phrases. If you are not sure of the meaning, look it up in the dictionary and write its definition.*

Word	Definition	Word	Definition
Cherokee		an owl	
common		a ritual	
a curse		a superstition	
hazardous		superstitious	
a journey		a symbol	
a lucky charm		vivid	

B *In the next unit, we will learn about superstitions from different countries. Think about your answers to these questions and write down some notes.*

1. What is an unlucky number in Japan?

_____

2. What do students in Japan do for good luck before exams?

_____

3. Do you believe in bad luck? Why or why not?

_____

4. Have you ever bought an *o-mamori*? Why did you buy it?

_____

5. Why do you think some people are superstitious?

_____

C *Exercise on expressing beliefs.*

If you are confident, say …	If you are unsure, say …
I believe …	I assume …
I feel …	I guess …
I know …	I imagine …
I think …	I suppose …

Examples

I don't believe that the number 13 is unlucky.
I suppose that an o-mamori might help you pass your exam.

Write two examples here

1. _____

2. _____

10 Superstitions

Learning Goal ☐ Expressing beliefs and abstract ideas

Warm-up

Look at the pictures below and answer the questions with your partner or group.

1. What are the five objects above?
2. Which ones are lucky? Which ones are unlucky?
3. Do you believe in any of these superstitions? Why or why not?
4. Is there anything you are superstitious about?

Vocabulary

Fill in the blanks with the vocabulary words from the Homework. You may need to change the form of the word to make it fit with the sentence.

1. I am a little bit _____, so I am always nervous on Friday the 13th.

2. Mount Fuji is sometimes a _____ for Japan. When people see it, they think of Japan.

3. Before the entrance exam, she went to the shrine and bought an *o-mamori*. She believed that the _____ helped her pass the test.

4. It is _____ to have *maneki neko* or "lucky cats" in restaurants. You can see them in many shops too.

5. It is _____ to drive a car while looking at your phone.

Reading

Pre-reading: You will read about superstitions in the country of Turkey. Talk with your partner or group and imagine what things Turkish people might be superstitious about. Share with the class.

Read: You have about ten minutes to read and answer the questions below. Then check your answers with your partner or group.

DL 38   CD 38

Superstitions in Turkey

A good luck charm
from Turkey

In Turkey, perhaps the most common superstition is about the "evil eye". The "evil eye" is when you look at someone with an angry face then something bad happens to them. Some people believe that someone with vivid green or blue eyes can give very powerful "evil eyes". Children often carry a blue glass bead as a lucky charm to protect themselves.

Another superstition is to pour water before someone leaves the house so that they will not have a hazardous journey. Also, people feel it is bad luck to pass someone scissors or knives—you should always set them down first and let the other person pick them up.

There are many superstitions about animals in Turkey. They believe that spiders in your house are good luck, so you should never kill them. However, they assume a black cat or an owl will bring bad luck.

There are some superstitions about numbers in Turkey. You will never see a house or hotel room with the number 13 because some believe it is the unluckiest number. The number 100 is also unlucky. This is because the word for 100 in Turkish sounds like the word for toilet. The number 40 is lucky, however. People imagine that if you say something forty times, it will become true.

1. What lucky charm do Turkish children carry? What does it protect them from?

_____

2. Why do people sometimes pour water before someone leaves the house?

_____

3. What animals are good luck? What animals are bad luck?

4. Why is the number 100 unlucky? Why do you think 40 is lucky?

5. Have you used something as a lucky charm?

6. What are some similar superstitions in Japan?

7. How do you think these superstitions started?

Discussion

Get with a partner and decide who is "A" and who is "B". Student A, go to page 107 and Student B, go to page 108. Read your text and answer the questions. Then explain the most important and interesting points to your partner. After that, have a group discussion using the questions below.

1. Are you superstitious? If yes, what about? If no, why not?

2. What do students do in Japan for good luck before exams?

3. Do you believe in curses? For example, they say that if someone enters an Egyptian pyramid, they will have something bad happen to them. Do you know of any famous curses?

4. What is an unlucky number in Japan? Do you have a lucky number?

5. Friday the 13th is considered by many people to be an unlucky day. Do you believe this? Are there any unlucky or lucky days in Japan?

6. Why do you think people are superstitious?

 Listening

You will hear Ryo, a Japanese university student, talking to Ama, his Cherokee friend. The Cherokee are a Native American people in North America. They are talking about superstitions and how colors can be symbols.

▌ *Pre-listening: Before you listen, talk to your partner about these questions.*

1. What do you know about Native American people in North America?

2. Are red and green symbols for something in Japan?

▌ *Listen: As you listen, fill in the chart. Then check your answer with your partner or group.*

🎧 DL 41   💿 CD 41

What does...	mean to the Cherokee?	mean to the Japanese?
an owl		
the number 4		
the number 7		
cedar and pine trees		
red		
blue		
white		
green		

Listen again and answer the questions. Check with your partner or group.

1. Is Ama nervous because it is Friday the 13th?

_____

2. Why is Ama superstitious about owls?

_____

3. Is the number 4 unlucky for the Cherokee? Why or why not?

_____

4. Ryo says the Japanese think something similar about trees. What does he mean?

_____

5. What is similar between Cherokee and Japanese beliefs?

_____

Discussion

Think about your answers to these questions. Then discuss them with your partner or group.

1. What do the colors red, blue, white, and green mean to you?
2. Are you superstitious about any animals, numbers, or colors?
3. Why do you think some colors have the same meanings in different cultures? (For example, in many countries, green is a symbol of life.)

Activity   Expressing beliefs and abstract ideas

With a partner, write a conversation about superstitions using the vocabulary, functions, and information you learned in this unit. Each person should have at least seven lines. Practice a few times, then perform in front of the class.

_____

_____

_____

_____

_____

_____

_____

_____

_____

_____

Homework for Unit 11

> Topic ● **Comparing cultures**
> Function ● **Talking about similarities**

A *Before the next lesson, you should understand the meanings of these words and phrases. If you are not sure of the meaning, look it up in the dictionary and write its definition.*

Word	Definition	Word	Definition
an altar		*fresh*	
an ancestor		*a kind of*	
to celebrate		*kind of*	
to decorate		*raw*	
a descendant		*to recommend*	
to dip		*to be similar*	
a dish	prepared food	*a special occasion*	
food	anything to eat		

B *In the next unit, we will learn about differences and similarities between cultures. Think about your answers to these questions and write down some notes.*

1. What is your favorite special occasion? Why do you like it?

_____

2. Write some notes about the food, decorations, activities, and clothes you wear on your favorite special occasion.

_____

3. Why do you think people in many different cultures celebrate birthdays?

_____

4. What are some ways holidays have changed since you were a child?

_____

C *Exercise on talking about similarities.*

Match the words and phrases below.

Okonomiyaki is … The weather in summer is … *Yukata* are … Autumn is … *O-bon* is …	different from the same as similar to	spring. fall. *monjayaki.* *kimono.* New Years.

Example

Okonomiyaki is similar to monjayaki because both are made with cabbage.

Write two examples here

1. _____

2. _____

Comparing Cultures

☐ Talking about similarities

Warm-up

With your partner or group, try to find three similar things for each pair below. Use the phrase "is/are similar to" like in the examples.

Examples *Dogs are similar to cats because they both have four legs, they both can be pets, and they are both covered in fur.*

dogs and cats	*okonomiyaki* and *monjayaki*	Osaka and Tokyo
kimono and yukata	high school and university	mikan and yuzu
coffee and tea	spaghetti and ramen	trains and busses
tennis and baseball	Christmas and New Years	K-pop and J-pop

Vocabulary

Fill in the blanks with the vocabulary words from the Homework. You may need to change the form of the word to make it fit with the sentence.

1. Sushi and sashimi are _____, but sushi is made with rice and sashimi is not.

2. My favorite _____ are Christmas and my birthday because I love to get presents.

3. _____ blueberries taste much better than frozen ones.

4. If you like spicy food, then I _____ eating Thai food. It is very spicy.

5. This curry is _____ spicy, but not too spicy.

Reading

Pre-reading: You will read about a Russian dish called "stroganina". It is made from raw fish. Talk with your partner or group and imagine this dish. What does it look like? How does it taste? What do people drink with it? Share with the class.

Read: You have about ten minutes to read and answer the questions below. Then check your answers with your partner or group.

DL 42   CD 42

Stroganina: the Siberian sashimi

In northern Russia, there is a unique dish called *stroganina*. It is similar to Japanese sashimi because it is made from raw fish. It is a little different from sashimi because it is frozen, sliced very thinly, and sometimes decorated with red onion and berries.

You do not need to use a fork or chopsticks to eat *stroganina*, just pick it up with your fingers. It is similar to sashimi because you dip it into something to add more flavor. Sashimi is dipped into soy sauce, but *stroganina* is dipped into salt and black pepper. Some people like to dip it into vinegar or oil flavored with herbs.

When you put the *stroganina* in your mouth, let it melt and enjoy the wonderful flavor. Then chew it slowly and enjoy the texture.

In Japan, some people like to drink tea or sake with sashimi. Similarly, Russians like to drink black tea or vodka with *stroganina*. *Stroganina* is a little expensive so people prefer to eat it only on special occasions like birthdays or at parties. It is best during the winter between December and February when the fish are fresh.

1. What are three similar things between sashimi and *stroganina*?

_____

2. How is *stroganina* different from sashimi?

_____

3. When do people usually eat *stroganina*?

_____

4. What food do you eat with your fingers? What food do you dip in salt or sauce?

_____

5. What kind of dishes do you eat only on special occasions or in the winter?

_____

Discussion

Get with a partner and decide who is "A" and who is "B". Student A, go to page 109 and Student B, go to page 110. Read your text and answer the questions. Then explain the most important and interesting points to your partner. After that, have a group discussion using the questions below.

1. What are the similarities between *O-bon* and the Day of the Dead?

2. What was interesting to you about these special occasions?

3. How do you usually celebrate *O-bon*?

 Listening

You will hear Akira talking to his Mexican friend, Veronica. Veronica tells Akira about how the Day of the Dead changed since she was a little girl.

▋ *Pre-listening: Before you listen, talk to your partner about these questions.*

1. What do you remember about the Day of the Dead from the last exercise?
2. How do you think the Day of the Dead has changed since the last generation?
3. How have Japanese holidays changed? Think of one example.

▋ *Listen: As you listen, put the following phrases in order.*   🎧 DL 45   💿 CD 45

	It's a celebration, it's fun.
1	It's a very important Mexican holiday.
	We're remembering family and friends who have died.
6	On the altar, she put candles, flowers, and photos of our family members…
	But the holiday has changed a lot since I was a kid.
	The graveyard was bright with candles.
	It's kind of sad my family doesn't do that anymore.
	We celebrated in a much more traditional way back then.
	My grandmother does something similar for *O-bon*.
	My family celebrated *O-bon* differently than now.

Listen again and answer the questions. Check with your partner or group.

1. Why and how do people celebrate the Day of the Dead?

_____

2. When Veronica was a child, where did she go to celebrate the Day of the Dead?

_____

3. How did Veronica's family celebrate the Day of the Dead when she was a child?

_____

4. Akira said his grandmother does something similar for *O-bon*. What do you think his grandmother does?

_____

5. Akira is going to tell Veronica about how he used to celebrate *O-bon* when he was a child. What are some things he might say?

_____

6. How do you and your family celebrate *O-bon*? How has this changed since you were a child?

_____

Discussion

Think about your answers to these questions. Then discuss them with your partner or group.

1. Tell your partner or group about the similarities between you and your best friend or you and someone in your family.

2. Think about clothes, food, music, language, and holidays in other countries. How are they similar to Japan?

3. The way we celebrate holidays changes over time. What is your opinion about these changes?

Activity | Talking about similarities

Write your answers to the questions below. Then ask two more people the same questions and write their answers. Find how many same or similar answers you have.

	Questions	Your answer	Partner 1	Partner 2	How many same or similar answers?
1	What is your name?				
2	What is your favorite food?				
3	What is your favorite drink?				
4	What is your favorite special occasion?				
5	Where do you usually eat lunch?				
6	Do you play a sport or a musical instrument?				
7	Have you been to Okinawa or Hokkaido?				
8	How old are you?				
9	How often do you ride the train?				
10	Can you ski or swim?				

71

Homework for Unit 12

Topic	Apologies
Function	Apologizing and forgiving

A *Before the next lesson, you should understand the meanings of these words and phrases. If you are not sure of the meaning, look it up in the dictionary and write its definition.*

Word	Definition	Word	Definition
to apologize		rude	
confident		sarcastic	
to forgive		similar / similarly	
modest		to tend to	to usually do something
odd	a little strange	trust	belief in someone
to offer		to be upset	
to restore			

B *In the next unit, we will learn about apologizing and forgiving. Think about your answers to these questions and write down some notes.*

1. When was the last time you apologized or you forgave someone? What happened?

   _____

2. How do you think apologizing might be different in other countries?

   _____

3. Can you think of an example of when a celebrity or politician apologized? What happened?

   _____

4. When you say *sumimasen*, is it always an apology or sometimes to say thank you?

   _____

C *Exercise on apologizing and forgiving.*

If you are apologizing, say ...	If you are forgiving someone, say ...
Sorry.	That's ok.
I'm sorry.	No problem.
Excuse me.	No need to apologize.
Pardon me.	I understand.
Forgive me.	I forgive you.

Examples

A: I'm sorry I'm late. The train stopped.   **B:** No need to apologize. I understand.

A: Forgive me for forgetting your birthday.   **B:** That's ok. I forgive you.

Write an example here

A: _____

B: _____

12 Apologies

Learning Goal ☐ Apologizing and forgiving

Warm-up

Look at the photos below and, using your imagination, answer the questions below with your partner or group.

1. a. Who are the two people in the first photo?
   b. Why is the man bowing? What are they saying to each other?

2. a. Who are the two people in the second photo?
   b. What is the man apologizing for? What are they saying to each other?

Vocabulary

Fill in the blanks with the vocabulary words from the Homework. You may need to change the form of the word to make it fit with the sentence.

1. You apologized for being late and I _____ you so I am not angry anymore.

2. After he lied to her, she did not believe anything he said. It took a long time to _____ her trust.

3. I think it is _____ that she did not text me back yesterday. It is a little strange, because she _____ write back immediately.

4. His English is almost perfect, but he is _____, so he says he cannot speak it very well.

5. When someone does something nice for you, it is _____ to not say thank you.

73

Reading

Pre-reading: You will read about apologizing in different cultures. Talk with your partner or group and imagine what might be similar and different in various countries. Share with the class.

Read: You have about ten minutes to read and answer the questions below. Then check your answers with your partner or group.

 DL 46 CD 46

Apologizing Across Cultures

We all make mistakes and apologize. Hopefully, we are forgiven. In different cultures, there are similarities and differences about when and how to apologize.

Researchers compared apologies in China, Korea, and the US. They discovered that all were similar in the way they apologize to friends. The difference was that Koreans apologize to strangers more than Chinese or Americans.

Other researchers looked at Japanese and American apologies. They found that both countries similarly use apologies to restore trust. However, Japanese tend to apologize even if it is not their fault. Americans tend to apologize only if it is their fault. This difference can cause misunderstandings between Japanese and Americans.

Also, in Japan, usually a simple apology is enough to restore trust. On the other hand, in America, after an apology, they often give an explanation, offer to do a favor, and then say something positive. For example, an American might apologize like this:

I'm sorry I'm late, but I got lost. I'll buy you lunch today, ok? Wow, what nice weather!

---

1. What is similar/different in the way Chinese, Koreans, and Americans apologize?

_____

2. What is the similar reason Japanese and Americans apologize?

_____

3. How are Japanese and American apologies different?

_____

4. What do you think about the American style of apologizing?

_____

5. What kind of misunderstandings might happen if Japanese and Americans apologize to each other?

_____

_____

Discussion

Get with a partner and decide who is "A" and who is "B". Student A, go to page 111 and Student B, go to page 112. Read your text and answer the questions. Then explain the most important and interesting points to your partner. After that, have a group discussion using the questions below.

1. In a speech, do you think it is more important to be apologetic and modest? Or is it more important to be confident? Why?

2. Why do you think apologizing is so important?

3. If someone is late meeting you, how do you think they should apologize?

4. If a waiter makes a mistake at a restaurant, how do you think they should apologize?

5. When tourists come to Japan, how might they be confused by the style of apologizing here?

 Listening

Adam, an American, was in the airport and a Japanese woman dropped her magazine. Adam picked it up for her and she apologized. Adam was a little confused, so he asks his Japanese friend, Yuki, about the situation.

| Pre-listening: Before you listen, talk to your partner about these questions.

1. Why do you think Adam was confused about the woman apologizing?

2. What do you think Yuki will tell him?

| Listen: As you listen, put the following phrases in order.  DL 49 CD 49

	"There's no need to apologize."
	In Japan, an apology doesn't always have a negative feeling
1	A Japanese woman dropped her magazine near me
	"Oh, I'm so sorry!"
	Communication is more than just words, isn't it?
	She should've just said, "Thanks."

Listen again and answer the questions. Check with your partner or group.

1. Why did Adam think the woman's apology was odd?

_____

2. What are some of the reasons Yuki gives for the woman's apology?

_____

3. What does Yuki mean when she says, "We should try to be empathetic"?

_____

4. If you were the woman in the airport, what would you say to Adam?

_____

5. In what situations does *sumimasen* mean "sorry" or "thank you"?

_____

6. What does Yuki mean when she asks, "are you being sarcastic?"

_____

Discussion

Think about your answers to these questions. Then discuss them with your partner or group.

1. When was the last time you apologized? Did the other person forgive you?
2. When is it difficult for you to apologize? When is it easy for you to apologize?
3. Do you find it easy or difficult to forgive people?
4. Can you think of an example of when a celebrity or politician apologized? What happened?
5. There is a saying, "Forgive and forget", but some people say, "Forgive, but never forget." What do these quotes mean to you? Which one do you agree with?

Activity   Apologizing and forgiving

Get with a partner. Take turns apologizing for the different situations below. Get with a second partner and do the exercise again, but faster to practice fluency.

Student A	Student B
Situation 1	
Your partner steps on your foot while getting on the train. Start the conversation by saying "Ouch!"	While getting on the train, you step on your partner's foot. Apologize.
Situation 2	
You borrowed your partner's book, but you lost it. Explain and apologize.	Your partner borrowed your book. You need it for class today. Start the conversation by asking "Do you have my book?"
Situation 3	
You are 30 minutes late to meet your partner. You could not text them because your phone had no battery. Apologize.	Your partner is 30 minutes late to meet you. They did not text you to tell you they were late. Start with "Where have you been?"
Situation 4	
You are a teacher. Your partner (a student) always forgets their homework. Start with "Do you have your homework?"	You are a student. You forgot to do your homework. Apologize to your teacher (your partner).

With a new partner, write a short conversation about apologizing for something. Try to use the phrases and vocabulary from this unit. Practice the conversation, then perform for the class.

Homework for Unit 13

|---|---|
| Topic | **Communication** |
| Function | **Using non-verbal communication / Arguing about a topic** |

A *Before the next lesson, you should understand the meanings of these words and phrases. If you are not sure of the meaning, look it up in the dictionary and write its definition.*

Word	Definition	Word	Definition
an argument		non-verbal	
to avoid		oral	
a context		a posture	
a gesture		a signal	
instantaneous		silence	
miscommunication			

B *In the next unit, we will learn about communication. Think about your answers to these questions and write down some notes.*

1. When you talk to someone in person, how far away are they from you?

2. Besides oral communication, what are some ways that people communicate?

3. What do you think is the best way to avoid miscommunication?

4. In a Japanese conversation, what can silence mean?

5. How do you think people will communicate in the future?

C *Exercise on arguing.*

If you are giving reasons, say …	If you are disagreeing, say …
The first reason …	That may be true, but …
The second reason …	That's a good point, but …
Another reason is …	Maybe, but the problem is …
The final reason is …	You may be right about … but …

Example

A: The first reason why speaking a foreign language is important is that it can help your career.

B: That may be true, but most people do not use a foreign language every day.

Write an example dialogue here

A: _____

B: _____

13 Communication

Learning Goal
- [ ] Using non-verbal communication
- [ ] Arguing about a topic

Warm-up

Look at the photos below and answer the following questions with your partner or group.

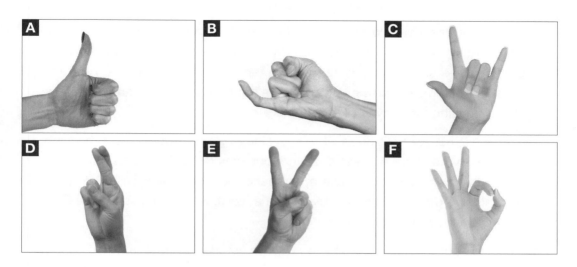

1. What is the meaning of the gesture in each of the photos?
2. What are some other ways of expressing the same meaning?
3. How could these gestures cause miscommunication?
4. What do you do when you do not understand something in class?

Vocabulary

Fill in the blanks with the vocabulary words from the Homework. You may need to change the form of the word to make it fit with the sentence.

1. If you take a quiz online, you can get _____ results.

2. Stand tall when you give a presentation. You need good _____.

3. Giving the "thumbs up" _____ is a form of _____ communication.

4. Some words have many meanings, but you can understand them by looking at the

   _____.

5. If you want to present a logical _____, give your reasons clearly.

 Reading

Pre-reading: You will read about non-verbal communication. Talk with your partner or group and discuss what are some ways that people communicate without using words. Share with the class.

Read: You have about ten minutes to read and answer the questions below. Then check your answers with your partner or group.

DL 50   CD 50

Non-Verbal Communication

You may not use words when you do non-verbal communication, but you say a lot. Whether we want to or not, we are always sending messages. These messages are sent by body language: facial expressions, eye contact, gestures, posture, and how much space we put between others and ourselves. As the old saying goes, even silence speaks louder than words.

We often use non-verbal signals while speaking to give our words more meaning. We use gestures, facial expressions, and tone of voice to punctuate our words. The words "thank you" can have a sarcastic meaning if said in a flat voice. Even when we do not know the meaning of a word, we can guess the meaning through non-verbal context.

We express our emotions more by the way we act than what we say. We cannot control all our non-verbal communication. For example, some people are "bad liars" because their body language shows that they are not being honest. Some people blush when they are embarrassed or surprised. A noisy stomach might tell others that we are hungry.

On the other hand, non-verbal communication can be the cause of miscommunication if people "read" the signals wrong. Someone may shiver from being cold, not from fear. While people from every culture use gestures, the meanings of the gestures are not universal. Giving eye contact might be important in one culture, but rude in another. Silence can have many meanings: I understand, I don't understand, I'm angry, or I'm thinking.

1. What are some examples of non-verbal communication?

_____

2. How is non-verbal communication used with verbal communication?

_____

3. What are some uncontrollable non-verbal signals?

_____

4. How can non-verbal communication lead to miscommunication?

_____

5. When do you use non-verbal signals?

_____

6. Have you ever miscommunicated with someone because of non-verbal communication?

_____

7. Do you agree with the quotation "silence speaks louder than words"? How do you use silence?

_____

Discussion

Get with a partner and decide who is "A" and who is "B". Student A, go to page 113 and Student B, go to page 114. Read your text and answer the questions. Then explain the most important and interesting points to your partner. After that, have a discussion using the questions below.

1. Which of the three points in A's story do you agree with the most, and why?
2. Which of the three points in A's story do you disagree with the most, and why?
3. Which of the three points in B's story do you agree with the most, and why?
4. Which of the three points in B's story do you disagree with the most, and why?
5. What is your opinion about learning a foreign language?

Listening

You will hear about the history of an important human invention for communication: writing.

▎*Pre-listening: Before you listen, talk to your partner about these questions.*

1. What comes to mind when you hear the word "technology"?
2. When do you use writing instead of speaking?

▎*Listen: As you listen, fill in the gaps with the missing phrases.*

🎧 DL 53   💿 CD 53

1	However, one of the most important _____ is not a machine at all.
2	Before writing, knowledge was passed to future generations _____ like stories and songs.
3	Writing made it possible to preserve and _____, send messages _____, and keep _____.
4	Writing _____ in different parts of the world.
5	Most of the writing used today evolved from these _____.

Listen again and answer the questions. Check with your partner or group.

1. According to the speaker, what is one of the most important pieces of technology?

_____

2. Why is oral tradition not always a good way to pass on information?

_____

3. What did writing make possible?

_____

Discussion

Think about your answers to these questions. Then discuss them with your partner or group.

1. How did you learn to write kanji?
2. What do you think Japanese writing will be like in the future?
3. How would your life be different if you could not read or write?

Activity   Arguing about a topic

You and your partner will argue two sides about one of the following topics:

- **Learning how to write kanji is not necessary.**
- **We should study more than one foreign language.**
- **Everyone in the world should speak the same language.**

Step 1 *In a group, think of four reasons to support your argument. Give examples to support your ideas.*

Your argument:

Reason 1 and why	
Reason 2 and why	
Reason 3 and why	
Reason 4 and why	

Step 2 *Listen to your partner's argument and write down their four reasons.*

Partner's argument:

Reason 1 and why	
Reason 2 and why	
Reason 3 and why	
Reason 4 and why	

Step 3 *Choose a reason you disagree with and why. Use the expressions in* C *of the Homework to respond to your classmate's reasons.*

Example   *You might be right about [Reason 2], but …*

Homework for Unit 14

Topic ● **Future Plans**

Function ● **Expressing speculation and possibilities**

A *Before the next lesson, you should understand the meanings of these words and phrases. If you are not sure of the meaning, look it up in the dictionary and write its definition.*

Word	Definition	Word	Definition
a colleague		an instrument	
be committed to		to involve	
to contribute		to market	to try to persuade people to buy products
an expert		particular	
to export		to refer to	
frequent		translation	

B *In the next unit, we will learn about talking about future plans. Think about your answers to these questions and write down some notes.*

1. What is your plan after graduation?

_____

2. What will Japan be like 20 years from now?

_____

3. Which country do you want to visit in the future and why?

_____

4. Have you read any science-fiction stories about the future? What did they say?

_____

5. What job is attractive to you and why?

_____

C *Exercise on expressing speculation and possibilities.*

If you are expressing speculation, say …	If you are expressing possibility, say …
It's likely/unlikely that … I suppose … I expect to … … be bound to … There's no way …	I might … It's possible … Perhaps … Maybe … Probably …

Example

It's unlikely that robots will take over all our jobs in the future.

Write two examples here

1. _____

2. _____

14 Future Plans

☐ Expressing speculation and possibilities

Warm-up

Discuss with your partner what you would do with one hundred million yen?
Read the following statements of university students and answer the questions.

Yoshiki I suppose I'd give all the money to an organization such as "Save The Children" which helps poor people in developing countries. I don't think spending all the money on myself is a good idea.

Jiwoo It's possible that the money would be gone soon. I have to be careful with money. I can't spend it like water, so I'd put 85 percent of the money in the bank.

Mika Perhaps I'd buy a house for my parents because I know that they've wanted one but that they can't afford it. It would be wonderful to make their dream come true.

Sue I lost my friend two years ago because of cancer. I know that scientists are bound to find a cure for cancer and I want to help them. So, I'd probably give most of the money to a cancer research organization.

Dan There's no way I'd spend all the money for shopping. I think I'd invest it. I'd buy lots of stocks and then live off the interest. I could be independent after school.

Ron I may sound selfish but I'd spend all the money on myself. You never know what will happen tomorrow, so I want to enjoy my life now. Probably I'd travel to see places.

1. Which idea do you most agree with and why?
2. Who wants to donate the money and why?
3. Who wants to save the money and why?
4. What would you do with the money?
5. Discuss your answers with a new partner.

Vocabulary

Fill in the blanks with the vocabulary words from the Homework. You may need to change the form of the word to make it fit with the sentence.

1. John is very _____ to his work.
2. We have been _____ in a plan to clean the park.
3. When you use this machine, please _____ the instructions on the paper.
4. I believe that medical research will _____ to a cure for cancer patients.
5. He is an _____ on zoology. He knows everything about animals.

 Reading

Pre-reading: You will read an essay written by Rina, who lived in Canada for 15 years. With your partner or group, discuss what she will write about her background and job. Share with the class.

Read: You have about ten minutes to read and answer the questions below. Then check your answers with your partner or group.

 DL 54   CD 54

My work

I am a *kikokushijo* (returnee). I was born in Canada, spent 15 years there and came back to Japan. Then I entered a Japanese university. I joined one of the university's rock bands as a keyboard player.

Since graduating from university, I have been working for a small company that makes digital musical instruments. I like this company because many of my colleagues chose this company due to their love of music. Even my middle-aged boss still plays in a band. The salary is not high so unless you are committed to music, you would not work here.

I am working in the area of marketing communication. As the company exports its products overseas, my job involves frequent use of English. Although I was not hired particularly for my English skills, my colleagues seem to refer to me as an English expert. They often ask me to check their English.

Whether you actually use particular English expressions or not in real life is something only those of us who have lived abroad can tell. That knowledge is something I can contribute to my company.

Although I like working at my company now, it is not likely that I will keep on working for this company forever. I am thinking of studying business but my future plans remain open at the moment.

1. What is Rina's background?

_____

2. Did you have "*kikokushijo*" classmates? What were they like?

_____

3. Why do you think Rina chose the company she is working at now?

_____

4. Why does Rina like her company?

_____

5. What does Rina do at her company?

_____

6. What do her colleagues ask her and why?

_____

7. Rina might change her jobs. Why do you think she might?

_____

8. Do you think you might change jobs in the future? Why or why not?

_____

Discussion

Get with a partner and decide who is "A" and who is "B". Student A, go to page 115 and Student B, go to page 116. Read your text and answer the questions. Then explain the most important and interesting points to your partner. After that, have a discussion using the questions below.

1. Do you have a strong motivation to study English? Why or why not?
2. Do you want to study abroad? Why or why not?
3. What are some benefits of studying abroad?
4. What classes have you enjoyed at university? Why are they interesting?
5. What is the best strategy to improve your English skills?
6. Is taking the Eiken test good for you? Why or why not?
7. What does being independent mean to you?
8. What made you decide to choose the university you study now?
9. What does being a professional mean?
10. What do you think is important in your future life?

 Listening

You will hear three people talking about their future plan.

❙ *Pre-listening: Before you listen, talk to your partner about these questions.*

1. What will you be doing in five years' time?
2. What job are you interested in and why?

❙ *Listen: As you listen, check ☑ what they talked about.* 🎧 DL 57 💿 CD 57

	Jobs they have now
	Teaching Japanese in Thailand
	Working at a car company in Germany
	Traveling around the world for fun
	Studying biology at university
	Eco-travel
	Helping to repair old buildings

Listen again and answer the questions. Check with your partner or group.

1. Who told Keiko that Thai students are eager to learn Japanese?

2. Why is studying Japanese popular in Thailand?

3. Susan says that teaching will suit Keiko. Why?

4. Where will Susan find a job?

5. What will Henry do after graduate school?

6. What is wrong with modern tourism?

7. What are some examples of ecological (green) holidays?

Discussion

Think about your answers to these questions. Then discuss them with your partner or group.

1. What helps university students to decide their future career?

2. What do you think about working for a foreign company?

3. What is your opinion about working overseas?

4. What is your opinion about ecological holidays, working holidays, homestay holidays and adventure holidays?

Activity | Expressing speculation and possibilities

Write a conversation between you and your friend using the vocabulary, functions, and information you learned in this unit about your future (10 years from now). Share your story with your group.

Reading
for Discussion

Memories and Experiences

Read the paragraph and answer the following questions. Be prepared to tell your partner the most important and interesting points.

 DL 07   CD 07

My school life

My name is Abbie. I was born in London and went to school there. At secondary school from 11 to 16 years old, compulsory subjects at school are English, Maths and Science. In the UK, when we turn 16, we decide whether to move up to the sixth form or go to a college. We can prepare for university at either sixth form or college or we  can choose to receive vocational education at college. I really liked history and wanted to study more about it at university in Manchester, so I went to sixth form. My friend Ken wanted to become a chef, so he went to college and received training. Now he works at an Italian restaurant in Manchester. Me and my university friends often go to the restaurant where Ken works to hang out. He is an excellent cook and we always enjoy eating there. I am still a student, but Ken is already a professional cook. I think it is amazing.

1. What are mandatory subjects at secondary school?

_____

2. What happens when you become 16 years old in the UK?

_____

3. At sixth form, what do students do?

_____

4. At college, what do students do?

_____

5. How does Abbie feel about Ken's being professional?

_____

6. What is your opinion about the UK system of education?

_____

Read the paragraph and answer the following questions. Be prepared to tell your partner the most important and interesting points. 🎧 DL 08 💿 CD 08

Mari's trip to Mexico

Mari took a Spanish class, which eventually helped her communicate in Spanish when she went to Mexico with her parents. She had thought she could make herself understood in English in Mexico because she believed that English was the common language in the world. The reality, however, was that local people in Mexico did not understand even simple English such as water or bus stop. Mari's Mexican experience changed her perception of the place of English. She realized that English was not always a tool for communication. Although she could not make herself understood in English,

Mari could communicate with the local people in Spanish she had begun to learn. She thought that learning multiple languages would help her communicate with more people in the world.

1. Who went to Mexico with Mari?

_____

2. What happened to Mari in Mexico?

_____

3. Before she went to Mexico, what had Mari thought about English?

_____

4. How did Mari communicate with local people in Mexico?

_____

5. If you cannot make yourself understood in English, what can you do?

_____

6. Have you had an experience similar to Mari's? What was it like?

_____

Food and Cooking

Read the recipe slowly while Student B takes notes. Then ask Student B the following questions.

DL 11 CD 11

"Dum Aloo"—a fantastic curry from northern India

Ingredients:

1 onion (chopped), 1 tablespoon olive oil, 2 potatoes (peeled and cut),
1 tablespoon coriander, 1 tablespoon chili powder, 1 tablespoon turmeric,
200g green peas, 220g canned tomatoes, salt, 120ml water.

Instructions:

First, fry onion in oil until tender (2 or 3 minutes).

Then, add potatoes and fry for about 5 minutes.

After that, sprinkle with coriander, chili powder, and turmeric.

Mix well and add peas.

Stir, add tomato, and season with salt.

Finally, add water, cover, and cook for 5 to 6 minutes until potatoes are tender.

Enjoy with rice or nan.

1. What is the name of this dish?

_____

2. What vegetables are in the curry?

_____

3. What is it seasoned with?

_____

4. How do you make it?

_____

5. Would you like to make this dish? Why or why not?

_____

6. Would you like to eat this dish? Why or why not?

_____

Read the recipe slowly while Student A takes notes. Then ask Student A the following questions.

DL 12   CD 12

"Hint of Mint"—an amazing fruit salad

Ingredients:

1 cup sugar, 1 cup water, 2½ cups chopped apples, 2½ chopped pears, 2 cups cubed pineapple, 2 cups sliced strawberries, 1 cup fresh blueberries, 1 cup mayonnaise, 1 teaspoon chopped fresh mint.

Instructions:

Put sugar and water into saucepan and boil.

Reduce heat and simmer* for 4 minutes.

Remove it from heat.

Add mint.

Cover and steep* for 20 minutes.

Take out mint.

Pour into small bowl and put it in refrigerator.

Before serving, combine apples, pears, pineapple, strawberries, and blueberries in a large bowl.

Stir mayonnaise into mint syrup then pour sauce over fruit.

Enjoy with hot or iced tea.

*simmer: below the boiling point
*steep: to put something in water to release its flavor

1. What is the name of this dish?

_____

2. What fruits are in the salad?

_____

3. What ingredients are in the sauce?

_____

4. How do you make the mint syrup?

_____

5. Would you like to make this dish? Why or why not?

_____

6. Would you like to eat this dish? Why or why not?

_____

Read the paragraph and answer the following questions. Be prepared to tell your partner the most important and interesting points.

 DL 15   CD 15

Allergies

An allergy is when the immune system, which protects the body from diseases, mistakes ordinary things in the environment as harmful to the body. Symptoms of allergic reactions include sneezing, coughing, runny nose, itchy eyes, and fatigue. Three common causes of allergies are animal dander*, dust, and pollen.

The first common cause is animal dander. Dander is dead skin cells from animals such as dogs, cats, and birds. Some people think getting a hairless dog or cat will make them less allergic, but they may continue to experience allergic reactions because these animals still have dander.

Another cause of allergies is pollen. Pollen allergy is called hay fever. Hay fever is seasonal, so people who suffer from it may experience it only at certain times of the year. Cedar and cypress trees are large producers of pollen, but people may be allergic to pollen from flower-making plants and grasses.

The final and most common cause of an allergic reaction is dust. Because dust is in houses, people who suffer from this type of allergy may have symptoms all year. A place can look clean and still have dust that might cause a reaction in some people. In fact, it is when people clean that dust scatters the most. Furthermore, dust mites, tiny animals that eat dust, may also cause allergic reactions making people's symptoms worse.

dander: flakes of skin

1. What does the immune system do?

_____

2. What are some symptoms of allergies?

_____

3. Why would hairless pets cause allergies?

_____

4. What is hay fever?

_____

5. Why would cleaning make dust allergies worse?

_____

Read the paragraph and answer the following questions. Be prepared to tell your partner the most important and interesting points. 🎧 DL 16 ◎ CD 16

Stress

Stress is the body's way of reacting to a physical or mental threat or challenge. Sometimes stress can motivate people to take on the challenge and overcome it. However, when stress becomes too strong and people cannot handle it, it can lead to serious physical and mental problems. There are three types of stress people might experience.

The first type of stress is "acute stress." This type of stress is the most common form and only lasts a short time. For example, someone might feel stress when the due date of an assignment is near, or if they must do a presentation. This stress disappears when the cause of the stress is finished.

The second type is "episodic acute stress." People who experience acute stress on a regular basis because they have many deadlines or other commitments may feel this type of stress. They could develop high blood pressure or heart disease if this stress is not released.

The final type of stress is "chronic stress." This is stress that people feel over a long period of time. People who are unhappy with their relationships or work, or people who suffer from events beyond their control, such as natural disasters or oppression, may feel this. It can lead to violent acts against themselves or others, or cause health problems like heart-related diseases.

1. What is stress?

_____

2. What could happen if people have too much stress?

_____

3. What is acute stress?

_____

4. What is episodic acute stress?

_____

5. What is chronic stress?

_____

Humans and Animals

Student **A**

Read the paragraph and answer the following questions. Be prepared to tell your partner the most important and interesting points.

DL 19   CD 19

Humans and Animals

Animals are similar to humans in many ways. They have friends and enemies, they have goals, they care about their family, they can be scared, they can relax, they can play, and they can dream.

Zoologists are researchers who watch animals for a long time. They see that each animal has its own unique personality. Like humans, some animals are outgoing, but others are shy. Some are violent, but others are kind. Some are lazy, and others work hard.

One interesting thing zoologists discovered about animals is that they can have empathy. There are many examples of animals helping each other and even helping humans. One time, in Africa, a woman was lost, and a group of elephants protected her while she slept at night. We often hear stories about dogs and even dolphins that help humans. Another example is a whale that saved a seal from being eaten by sharks.

When we understand how similar we are to animals, maybe we will stop being cruel to them.

---

1. How are humans and animals similar?

_____

2. What do zoologists know about animals' personalities?

_____

3. What is an example of animals having empathy?

_____

4. If we understand that we are similar to animals, we will not be cruel to them. Do you agree? Why or why not?

_____

5. Have you ever seen animals (pets, in a zoo, in nature) acting like humans?

_____

6. What is an interesting, funny, or frightening experience you had with an animal?

_____

Read the paragraph and answer the following questions. Be prepared to tell your partner the most important and interesting points.

 DL 20   CD 20

Working with Animals

I love animals. I could be a vet, but I am not interested in medicine. I did some research and found that there are many kinds of jobs involving animals. Here are my top 4 choices:

❶ **Zoologist**
Zoologists work in zoos, but sometimes work in nature. They research animal behavior. I want to be a zoologist researching elephants in Thailand.

❷ **Animal Trainer**
Trainers teach animals how to act in movies. They also train seeing-eye dogs. This is a fantastic job because I could meet famous actors or help blind people.

❸ **Animal Cruelty Investigator**
Investigators work with the police to save animals from cruel people who hurt them. I am interested in solving crimes and helping animals, so this is the perfect job.

❹ **Dog Walker**
Many dogs are at home alone while their owners are at work. Dog walkers take these lonely dogs for a walk. This is probably the easiest job, so I will start my career by being a dog walker.

1. Where does the author want to be a zoologist?

_____

2. What is a seeing-eye dog?

_____

3. Why is job ❸ the perfect job for the author?

_____

4. Why does the author think that being a dog walker is the easiest job?

_____

5. Which job do you like the best? Why? Which job do you not want to do? Why?

_____

6. What other kinds of jobs are there with animals?

_____

Read the paragraph and answer the following questions. Be prepared to tell your partner the story.

 DL 23   CD 23

An Embarrassing Mistake

Steve, a young Canadian, moved to Japan in 1997 to work. He could not read or speak any Japanese and there were very few English signs in Tokyo then. He stayed at a hotel in Shinjuku and wanted to take the train to Harajuku. When he went to Shinjuku Station, he did not understand how to buy a ticket, so he decided to watch people and see how they did it. He walked over to an old man at a machine and saw him put money in a slot, push a button, and a ticket came out. Steve could not read what the buttons said, so he decided to just buy any ticket then have the staff at Harajuku Station help him.

First, he put some money into the machine, then pushed a button, and finally a ticket came out. He put his ticket into the gate, but it suddenly closed, and an alarm sounded. He was very surprised and did not know what to do. A station attendant in a bright blue uniform came over to his gate, opened it, and pulled out his ticket. The attendant looked at Steve's ticket, suddenly started laughing, and said, "*Ra-men! Ra-men!*" while pointing to the ramen shop nearby. Steve almost died of embarrassment once he realized he had bought a ticket for ramen and not a train. Luckily, the kind attendant helped him buy the right ticket and Steve went to Harajuku.

---

1. Who are the characters in this story? What do they look like? How do they act?

_____

2. What is the setting of this story? Describe it.

_____

3. What was the problem? How did the main character feel?

_____

4. How did the story end?

_____

5. Steve made more embarrassing mistakes when he went to Harajuku. What do you think happened?

_____

6. Have you or someone you know done something embarrassing?

_____

Read the paragraph and answer the following questions. Be prepared to tell
your partner the story.

🎧 DL 24   ◎ CD 24

A Frightening Bus Ride

One time, when I was in junior high school, I came home really late
because I was studying at a friend's house. By the time I got back to my train
station, it was almost midnight. I got on the bus to go home and there were
not many people on it. Just the driver, two high school students in uniforms,
and a bald businessman in a blue suit.

At the first stop the students got off. Then, at the next stop, the businessman
got off. At the stop after that, an elderly couple got on. They were very pale
and wore old-fashioned clothing. As they walked to the back of the bus, I
noticed that they smelled like eggs and smoke. It seemed very strange and
I felt uncomfortable. I could hear the old couple whispering and although I
could not understand them, the way they spoke made me nervous.

Luckily, the bus came to my stop and I quickly walked towards the exit.
Just before I exited the bus, I looked at the couple and, you will never believe

what happened, but they were not there!
They had disappeared! I was scared to
death. I ran all the way home and told my
parents that I had seen two ghosts on the
bus. They just laughed at me and said it was
my imagination. However, I feel confident
that what I saw was real.

1. Who are the characters in this story? What do they look like? How do they act?

_____

2. What is the setting of the story?

_____

3. What did the main character see, smell, and hear on the bus?

_____

4. How did the main character feel? How does this story make you feel?

_____

5. Do you think this is a true story?

_____

6. Do you know any ghost stories?

_____

Read the paragraph and answer the following questions. Be prepared to tell your partner the most important and interesting points.

 DL 27   CD 27

Pet Peeves

A "pet peeve" is an action that we find particularly annoying. Other people may experience the same action and do not have a bad feeling about it. However, to the person with the pet peeve, it is extremely frustrating.

Pet peeves can be caused by two emotions. The first one is irritation. If we think someone's actions are bad, we may feel angry about them. Some common pet peeves in this category are people cutting lines instead of going to the end of it, groups of people walking slowly and taking up all the space on the sidewalk, and people talking loudly on the telephone.

The second emotion is disgust. We may think some people's actions are unpleasant or offensive. Actions such as chewing food loudly, not cleaning after your dogs on the street, or not covering your mouth when you cough make some people feel disgusted.

Some people dislike certain sounds. If the sounds are high, they can be especially annoying. Fingernails moving across a blackboard, babies crying on an airplane, or cats meowing at night are examples of this. Sometimes we do not like a word because of its meaning. Some people dislike the word "moist" because they have a negative image of the word, but these same people may not react at all to words with similar meanings like "damp" or "wet", or words that describe things that are more unpleasant, like "sickness".

1. What is a pet peeve?

_____

2. What are the two emotions that cause pet peeves?

_____

3. What are some examples of the first type?

_____

4. What are some examples of the second type?

_____

5. Why do people dislike certain sounds?

_____

Read the paragraph and answer the following questions. Be prepared to tell your partner the most important and interesting points.

 DL 28   CD 28

Phobias

Phobias are exaggerated or irrational fears of animals, objects, places, or situations. They are usually caused by stressful or fearful experiences during childhood but may also develop as late as early adulthood. Some phobias are learned. For example, if a child sees that their parent is afraid of spiders, arachnophobia, the child might also develop this fear.

Phobias can be put into three groups. The first group is "specific phobia." This is a fear of a specific object or situation. The fears of snakes, heights, and blood are in this category. In most cases the object or situation that causes the fear can be easily avoided.

The second group of phobias is "social phobia." This is the fear of being negatively judged by others or being publicly embarrassed. Someone may feel this while being introduced, speaking in front of a large group of people, or meeting people in authority. Some people with social phobia do not feel comfortable eating with others.

The final group of phobias is "agoraphobia." Agoraphobia means a fear of open spaces, but it may also mean a fear of crowded places, or the fear of being outside the home. People with this phobia find it difficult to ride public transportation, go to stadiums or theaters, or wait in long lines.

Social phobia and agoraphobia seem similar in the sense that they may cause people to avoid crowds and stay inside their homes. However, the difference between these two types is whether there are interactions with people or not.

1. What is a phobia and what are the causes of phobias?

_____

2. What is a specific phobia? Give some examples.

_____

3. What is a social phobia? Give some examples.

_____

4. How are social phobia and agoraphobia similar? How are they different?

_____

5. If you have a phobia, how do you think you can overcome it?

_____

Read the paragraph and answer the following questions. Be prepared to tell your partner the most important and interesting points.

 DL 35   CD 35

Blood type

Some people believe that blood type tells a person's personality.

Type A's are organized and like things to be done perfectly. Their rooms are always clean and tidy. They can be stubborn and get stressed out easily. They also value harmony with others.

Type B's are relaxed and say what they think. They have strong curiosity and can concentrate only on things that interest them and lose interest easily.

Type O's can get along with everybody and are good problem solvers. They are confident and optimistic and have leadership abilities. They do not care about little things but they are flexible.

Type AB's tend to be creative. Many geniuses are said to come from the AB group. They are often seen as dual-natured and complicated. For example, they are shy but also are outgoing.

Which blood type do you have?

1. What do blood type A people like?

_____

2. Which blood type people can be good problem solvers?

_____

3. What personalities do blood type AB's have?

_____

4. Which blood type people are relaxed?

_____

5. Which blood type do you have?

_____

6. Make your own question.

_____

Read the paragraph below. Then ask your partner the following questions.
Be prepared to tell your partner the most important and interesting points.

 DL 36  CD 36

Favorite color

What color do you wear often? A quick look at the colors of the clothes can help you find out what you are.

According to color psychology, your favorite color defines your personality. To define your favorite color, you may look for patterns of choices of clothing or decorative items.

Red people have strong will and energy. They want many different things in life.

Blue people have a peaceful personality and desire to live according to principles.

Green people want to have safety and security. They need to be loved.

People wearing yellow are optimistic about life and they are dreamers.

Wearing brown means they enjoy a simple life and good friends. They are friendly.

People who wear black are independent and strong-willed.

Grey people may have few or no opinions. They may hide their emotions from others.

Orange people can be described as social butterflies. They love people and like to be around others.

1. What does our favorite color define?

_____

2. How can we find our favorite color?

_____

3. Which color types are similar and how?

_____

4. Which color type may like parties and why?

_____

5. What does "social butterflies" mean?

_____

6. Make your own question.

_____

Read the paragraph and answer the following questions. Be prepared to tell your partner the most important and interesting points.

DL 39   CD 39

Superstition in Baseball

In America, baseball players and fans are particularly superstitious. A long time ago, baseball players believed that seeing white horses before a game meant good luck. The manager of the New York Giants paid a man to ride a white horse in front of his team before each game.

These days numbers are lucky. Players will request their lucky number for their uniform. Also, many people do rituals—for example, some players always eat fried chicken prior to a game and others do not wash their uniforms until the day after a game. They imagine that doing these rituals will bring them good luck.

Many people think the Boston Red Sox were cursed after the famous player Babe Ruth left the team. After he left, the Red Sox did not win the World Series for 86 years.

1. A long time ago, how did baseball players get good luck?

2. These days, how do baseball players get good luck?

3. What happened after Babe Ruth left the Boston Red Sox?

4. Are there any superstitions in baseball in Japan?

5. What do people in Japan do for good luck?

6. Do you know of any curses, lucky numbers, or rituals?

Read the paragraph and answer the following questions. Be prepared to tell your partner the most important and interesting points.

 DL 40 CD 40

Lucky Charms

In many countries, people believe that a rabbit's foot is lucky (but not lucky for the rabbit). Rabbits' feet are made into key chains and people imagine it will give them good luck.

In other cultures, people think that a horseshoe above a door will help keep bad luck out and keep good luck in the room.

Four-leaf clovers are very rare—about one in 10,000. Perhaps this is why people think you will have good luck if you find a four-leaf clover. It is also a symbol for the country of Ireland.

In Japan, the *o-mamori* is a lucky charm that people believe protects them from various hazards. It should never be opened, or it will lose its luck.

1. Have you seen a rabbit's foot lucky charm? Would you like one? Why or why not?

_____

2. What lucky charm do people put over their door for good luck?

_____

3. Why do people think four-leaf clovers are good luck?

_____

4. Do you have an *o-mamori*? Do you have any other lucky charms?

_____

5. What do people in Japan do for good luck?

_____

Comparing Cultures

Read the paragraph and answer the following questions. Be prepared to tell your partner the most important and interesting points.

 DL 43   CD 43

O-Bon

This special occasion is usually held around August 15th and is to remember ancestors. People put food, flowers, and candles on an altar. The weather is often very hot, so some people wear a light cotton *kimono* called "yukata". They eat summer foods like watermelon and somen (cold noodles). People visit graves and light candles for their ancestors. They put fresh fruit and sake on the graves for the spirits of their family. The largest *Bon Odori* festivals overseas are in Brazil and California where many Japanese descendants live.

1. Why do people in Japan celebrate *O-bon*?

_____

2. How do people prepare altars?

_____

3. What do people wear during *O-bon*?

_____

4. What do people do?

_____

5. Is *O-bon* celebrated abroad? Where?

_____

Comparing Cultures

Student **B**

Read the paragraph and answer the following questions. Be prepared to tell your partner the most important and interesting points.

 DL 44 CD 44

Day of the Dead

This special occasion is usually held around November 1st and is a holiday to remember ancestors. People decorate altars with food, flowers, and candles. People always wear their best clothes like suits, dresses, and new shoes. They eat *pan dulce* (a kind of sweet bread) and *calaveras* (candy skulls). People visit graves and light candles for their ancestors. They put fresh fruit and tequila on the graves for the spirits of their family. The largest Day of the Dead festivals outside Mexico are in California and Texas where many Mexican descendants live.

1. Why do people in Mexico celebrate the Day of the Dead?

_____

2. How do people decorate altars?

_____

3. What do people wear during the Day of the Dead?

_____

4. What do people do?

_____

5. Is the Day of the Dead celebrated outside of Mexico? Where?

_____

Read the paragraph and answer the following questions. Be prepared to tell your partner the most important and interesting points.

 DL 47   CD 47

Modesty or Confidence?

At an international business conference, people from many different countries gave presentations in English. Below are the opening lines of four different speeches. In your opinion, which ones are better? Why?

Speech A	Speech B
I am sorry my English is not very good, but please try to understand my presentation.	I have been a manager at my company for 25 years and I am an expert in employee motivation.

Speech C	Speech D
Today, I will teach you some amazing skills that will definitely improve your career.	This topic is difficult, so forgive me if I make a mistake. Hopefully you can learn something from my speech.

After each speech, the audience answered a questionnaire. Japanese people preferred speeches A and D. Americans preferred speeches B and C. Why? The Japanese audience said speakers A and D were apologetic and modest, so they felt more comfortable listening to them. The Americans said speakers B and C were confident, so they felt like they could learn more from them.

1. What is similar between speeches A and D? Between B and C?

_____

2. Which speech opening do you prefer? Why?

_____

3. Which speech opening do you not like? Why?

_____

4. Do you think it is true that Japanese prefer to listen to an apologetic and modest speaker? Why or why not?

_____

5. Do you think it is possible to be both confident and modest? How?

_____

Unit 12 Apologies

Read the paragraph and answer the following questions. Be prepared to tell your partner the most important and interesting points.

DL 48   CD 48

The Late Tour Guide

A group of elderly Japanese tourists were staying at a hotel in New York City. On the first morning, they met in the hotel lobby to start a tour at 9:00. All of the tourists arrived before 8:50, but the American tour guide was not there. By 9:15 the tourists were nervous and a little upset. The tour guide ran into the lobby at 9:20 and said, "Good morning everyone! Sorry, but the subway was stopped and I couldn't get a taxi so I had to run all the way here. Anyway, we're going to have a lot of fun today so let's go!"

The tourists were even more upset and thought that the tour guide was rude. When they complained to the tour company owner, the owner sincerely apologized, told them he would retrain the guide, and gave the tourists a 10% discount at a souvenir shop.

1. How upset would you be if your tour guide was twenty minutes late?

2. Why did the tourists think the tour guide was rude? Do you think the tour guide was rude? Why or why not?

3. What do you think the tour guide should have said?

4. How do you think the tour company will retrain the tour guide?

5. What kind of cultural misunderstanding do you think happened?

Read the paragraph and answer the following questions. Be prepared to tell your partner the most important and interesting points.

 DL 51 CD 51

Studying a Foreign Language is Important

We must study literature, math, and science to get a full education, and learning a foreign language is just as important. Learning a language is hard, and there may be easier things to do, but learning a foreign language is necessary to improve your success in life.

The first reason is that learning a foreign language makes you a citizen of the world. You would have more opportunities to make friends from various countries and learn about different cultures. You can see the world through different points of view.

The second reason is that it will make you more desirable to companies. Technology has made the world a smaller place, and rather than having just a local customer base, some customers can be on the other side of the world. People who can speak the customer's language would be more attractive than someone who cannot.

The final reason is that learning a foreign language makes you smarter. Having a different worldview makes problem solving easier. Also, it stimulates your brain, which improves memory and keeps it healthy while you age.

Learning a foreign language might be hard for some people, but there are many good benefits that make it worth it.

1. Why does the writer think it is important to learn a foreign language?

2. What is the first reason why people should study another language?

3. What are the second and third reasons?

4. Which of these three points do you agree with the most, and why?

5. Which of these three points do you disagree with the most, and why?

6. What is your opinion about learning a foreign language?

Read the paragraph and answer the following questions. Be prepared to tell your partner the most important and interesting points.

DL 52   CD 52

Studying a Foreign Language is Not Necessary

Governments, schools, and companies say that learning a foreign language is important and they make rules to make you study. I can understand why learning a foreign language can be helpful, but I do not think learning a foreign language is necessary.

The first reason is that it is not needed in daily life. In Japan, everyone speaks one language. Most people do not use a foreign language at work, and few people travel abroad. You can live your life without ever needing to know another language.

Another reason why learning a language is not necessary is because translation technology is getting better and better. Some software gives you instantaneous translations, so you can read signs or have conversations with someone who does not speak your language without difficulty.

The final reason is that learning a foreign language takes a lot of time and effort. If you do not have to study a language, you would have more free time to do more interesting things, like taking classes you like, or spending more time on a hobby, or with friends.

Learning a foreign language could be fun for those who want to, but not everyone needs to study it.

---

1. What does the writer think about learning foreign languages?

_____

2. What is the first reason why people do not need to learn a foreign language?

_____

3. What are the second and third reasons?

_____

4. Which of these three points do you agree with the most, and why?

_____

5. Which of these three points do you disagree with the most, and why?

_____

6. What is your opinion about learning a foreign language?

_____

Future Plans

Read the paragraph and answer the following questions. Be prepared to tell your partner the most important and interesting points.

DL 55   CD 55

Letter to my teacher

Dear Mr. Yamamoto,

It has been a while since I graduated from Hakone High School. I have been enjoying my university life. So far, I have taken basic subjects and mandatory subjects. In the second semester, though, I suppose I will take classes with specific contents of my major, Cultural Studies.

I believed that I would never be good at English until I studied abroad, but recently I have started studying English by myself. At university, I am supposed to take "English Communication" class but I do not have to take it because I passed Eiken 2nd grade.

To tell the truth I started studying English by myself because of my experience of talking with an American student who did not speak Japanese at all. I had difficulties speaking English with him and I was mortified at the incident. That experience was a trigger for me to start studying English.

Look forward to seeing you soon.

Best regards,
Yuji Saito

1. What does Yuji do now?

2. What is Yuji's major?

3. What did Yuji believe about learning English?

4. Why does Yuji not take English Communication?

5. Why did Yuji start learning English by himself?

6. Do you have an experience that motivated you to learn English?

Read the paragraph and answer the following questions. Be prepared to tell your partner the most important and interesting points.

 DL 56   CD 56

Story of my life

My name is Sue. I was born in Myanmar and came to Japan with my family when I was 14. I went to a junior high school in Yokohama. I could not speak Japanese, so I took Japanese lessons after school every day. I wanted to become independent in the future, so I wanted to become a professional in some area as I strongly believed that a professional skill would help me in the future. I had a strong desire to help people. My options were to become a nurse, a care-giver, or a medical technician. I chose the third one and decided to be a radiologist. After struggling to determine what I wanted to be, I found a university that had a program I was interested in. Now I am studying to become a radiologist. I hope I will gain experience working in hospitals overseas.

1. When did Sue come to Japan?

_____

2. How did Sue learn Japanese?

_____

3. What three choices did Sue have as a future career?

_____

4. What does Sue want to be in the future and why?

_____

5. What is Sue's future hope?

_____

6. To become what you want in the future, how will you prepare?

_____

本書には CD（別売）があります

Bridging Communication Skills

基礎から発信への英語コミュニケーションスキル

2019 年 3 月 31 日　初版第 1 刷発行
2022 年 9 月 5 日　初版第 5 刷発行

著　者　　鈴　木　　栄
Matthew Miller
Patrick McClue

発行者　　福　岡　正　人
発行所　　株式会社　金星堂

（〒 101-0051）東京都千代田区神田神保町 3-21
Tel. (03) 3263-3828（営業部）
(03) 3263-3997（編集部）
Fax (03) 3263-0716
http://www.kinsei-do.co.jp

編集担当　今門貴浩　　　　　　　　　　　　Printed in Japan
印刷所・製本所／株式会社カシヨ
ISBN978-4-7647-4091-4　C1082

Writing
Tasks

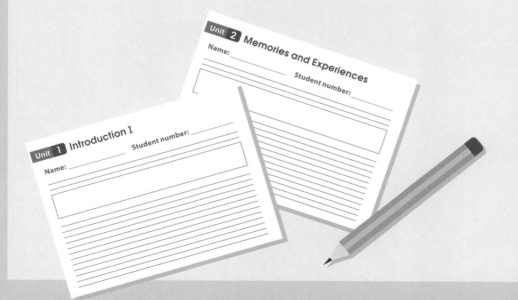

Unit 1 Introduction I

Name: _____ **Student number:** _____

Your teacher will ask you to write about one of the topics below. Write a paragraph in English using the vocabulary and phrases from the unit. You can write on the back of the page if you need more space.

1. One of your partners from the class
2. Your self-introduction
3. A message to your teacher about what you want to learn in this class

_____

_____

_____

_____

_____

_____

_____

_____

_____

Unit 2 Memories and Experiences

Name: _____ **Student number:** _____

Your teacher will ask you to write about one of the topics below. Write a paragraph in English using the vocabulary and phrases from the unit. You can write on the back of the page if you need more space.

1. Your high school
2. Your favorite teacher
3. Your opinion about entrance exams

_____

_____

_____

_____

_____

_____

_____

_____

_____

Unit 3 Food and Cooking

Name: _____ **Student number:** _____

Your teacher will ask you to write about one of the topics below. Write a paragraph in English using the vocabulary and phrases from the unit. You can write on the back of the page if you need more space.

1. Your favorite dish
2. How to make a rice ball
3. Your opinion about dieting

_____
_____
_____
_____
_____
_____
_____
_____
_____

Unit 4 Health

Name: _____ **Student number:** _____

Your teacher will ask you to write about one of the topics below. Write a paragraph in English using the vocabulary and phrases from the unit. You can write on the back of the page if you need more space.

1. What you do to stay healthy
2. The best way to relieve stress
3. Advice about exercise

_____
_____
_____
_____
_____
_____
_____
_____

Unit 5 Humans and Animals

Name: _____ **Student number:** _____

Your teacher will ask you to write about one of the topics below. Write a paragraph in English using the vocabulary and phrases from the unit. You can write on the back of the page if you need more space.

1. Your pet
2. Why you like/do not like zoos
3. Your opinion about vegetarianism

_____

_____

_____

_____

_____

_____

_____

_____

_____

Unit 6 Telling Stories

Name: _____ **Student number:** _____

Your teacher will ask you to write about one of the topics below. Write a paragraph in English using the vocabulary and phrases from the unit. You can write on the back of the page if you need more space.

1. Your favorite story as a child
2. A ghost story
3. Something funny, interesting, embarrassing, or frightening that happened to you

_____

_____

_____

_____

_____

_____

_____

_____

Unit 7 Emotions

Name: _____ **Student number:** _____

Your teacher will ask you to write about one of the topics below. Write a paragraph in English using the vocabulary and phrases from the unit. You can write on the back of the page if you need more space.

1. Your happiest memory
2. What you do when someone annoys you
3. What you do when you feel confused in class

_____
_____
_____
_____
_____
_____
_____
_____

Unit 8 Introduction II

Name: _____ **Student number:** _____

Your teacher will ask you to write about one of the topics below. Write a paragraph in English using the vocabulary and phrases from the unit. You can write on the back of the page if you need more space.

1. One of your partners' summer vacations
2. Your summer vacation
3. What you want to do next summer vacation

_____
_____
_____
_____
_____
_____
_____
_____

Unit 9 Intelligence

Name: _____ **Student number:** _____

Your teacher will ask you to write about one of the topics below. Write a paragraph in English using the vocabulary and phrases from the unit. You can write on the back of the page if you need more space.

1. Your favorite color
2. Why you like/do not like sports
3. Your opinion about judging people by blood type

_____
_____
_____
_____
_____
_____
_____
_____

Unit 10 Superstitions

Name: _____ **Student number:** _____

Your teacher will ask you to write about one of the topics below. Write a paragraph in English using the vocabulary and phrases from the unit. You can write on the back of the page if you need more space.

1. Something you are superstitious about
2. Your lucky number, or lucky charm
3. Why you think people are superstitious

_____
_____
_____
_____
_____
_____
_____
_____

Unit 11 Comparing Cultures

Name: _____ **Student number:** _____

Your teacher will ask you to write about one of the topics below. Write a paragraph in English using the vocabulary and phrases from the unit. You can write on the back of the page if you need more space.

1. Your favorite holiday
2. Similarities between Japan and another country
3. How holidays have changed since you were a child

_____
_____
_____
_____
_____
_____
_____
_____
_____

Unit 12 Apologies

Name: _____ **Student number:** _____

Your teacher will ask you to write about one of the topics below. Write a paragraph in English using the vocabulary and phrases from the unit. You can write on the back of the page if you need more space.

1. The last time you apologized to someone
2. The last time you forgave someone
3. What you know about how people apologize in other countries

_____
_____
_____
_____
_____
_____
_____
_____

Unit 13 Communication

Name: _____   **Student number:** _____

Your teacher will ask you to write about one of the topics below. Write a paragraph in English using the vocabulary and phrases from the unit. You can write on the back of the page if you need more space.

1. What happened when you miscommunicated with a friend
2. Which is better, talking on the phone or sending text messages
3. To what level of proficiency students should study a foreign language

_____
_____
_____
_____
_____
_____
_____
_____
_____

Unit 14 Future Plans

Name: _____   **Student number:** _____

Your teacher will ask you to write about one of the topics below. Write a paragraph in English using the vocabulary and phrases from the unit. You can write on the back of the page if you need more space.

1. Your future job
2. Your role model
3. Money

_____
_____
_____
_____
_____
_____
_____
_____
_____